A Unique Relationship

A Unique Relationship

The United States and the Republic of China Under the Taiwan Relations Act

Edited by
Ramon H. Myers

Hoover Institution Press

Stanford University

Stanford, California

Hoover Press Publication 387

First printing, 1989
95   94   93   92   91   90   89   9   8   7   6   5   4   3   2   1
Simultaneous first paperback printing, 1989
95   94   93   92   91   90   89   9   8   7   6   5   4   3   2   1

Manufactured in the United States of America

Printed on acid-free paper

Library of Congress Cataloging in Publication Data

A Unique relationship : the United States and the Republic of China under the Taiwan Relations Act / edited by Ramon H. Myers.
          p.   cm.
   Bibliography: p.
   Includes index.
   ISBN 0–8179–8871–8 (alk. paper).
   ISBN 0–8179–8872–6 (pbk. : alk. paper)
   1. United States—Foreign relations—Taiwan. 2. Taiwan—Foreign relations—United States.   I. Myers, Ramon Hawley, 1929–   .
JX1428.T34U54   1989   89–15411
327.7305124'9—dc20   CIP

Contents

Editor's Preface

BY EDITORIAL PREFERENCE, all Chinese personal names and place-names (except Beijing) have been romanized according to the Wade-Giles format, with the Chinese surname cited first as in ordinary Chinese usage.

The editor gratefully acknowledges the financial support of the Hoover Institution on War, Revolution and Peace for sponsoring the conference in September 1988 that made possible this collection of essays. The views presented below are neither endorsed by nor representative of the Hoover Institution. All errors and omissions are the responsibility of the editor.

United States government officials are compelled, under the Taiwan Relations Act, to refer to the Chinese state on Taiwan as Taiwan instead of the Republic of China. Private citizens, however, reserve the right to describe the real world. Two Chinese states have ruled different territories since 1949, but each still claims sovereignty over the territory governed by the other. Moreover, very different societies and political systems have evolved under these two Chinese states. For these reasons, all except chapter 2 refer to these Chinese states by their appropriate names: the People's Republic of China and the Republic of China.

Contributors

RICHARD BUSH serves as a staff consultant for the Subcommittee on Asian and Pacific Affairs of the Committee on Foreign Affairs of the House of Representatives. Before assuming that position in 1983, he was on the staff of The Asia Society's China Council. He received a Ph.D. in political science from Columbia University and is the author of *The Politics of Cotton Textiles in Kuomintang China, 1927–1937.*

DAVID S. CHOU is Associate Professor and Deputy Director, Institute of International Relations, National Chengchi University. He received his Ph.D. from Duke University and has written extensively on international affairs.

RALPH N. CLOUGH is a Professorial Lecturer and Coordinator of the SAIS China Forum at the School of Advanced International Studies, The Johns Hopkins University, Washington, D.C. He is a retired Foreign Service Officer who was Director for Chinese Affairs in the Department of State and served abroad in China, Hong Kong, and Taiwan. He was Deputy Chief of mission at the U.S. Embassy in Taiwan from 1961 to 1965. He is the author of *East Asia and U.S. Security* (1975), *Deterrence and Defense in Korea: The Role of U.S. Forces* (1976), *Island China* (1978), and *Embattled Korea: The Rivalry for International Support* (1987).

HARVEY FELDMAN recently retired from the U.S. Foreign Service after a 32-year career as an Asian specialist. He was Director of Republic of China Affairs during the period of normalization of relations with the PRC and later served as one of the American ambassadors to the UN in New York. He has written extensively on contemporary Taiwan and is the editor of *Taiwan in a Time of Transition*, published earlier this year by Paragon Press. Ambassador Feldman is now Director of International Relations for the American Jewish Committee.

RAMON H. MYERS is Senior Fellow and Curator-Scholar of the East Asian Collection of the Hoover Institution on War, Revolution and Peace at Stanford, California. Formerly Associate Editor of *The Journal of Asian Studies* and Editor of *Ch'ing-shih wen-ti*, he coedited with Mark R. Peattie *The Japanese Colonial Empire 1895–1945* (1983) and with Peter Duus and Mark R. Peattie *The Japanese Informal Empire in China, 1895–1937* (1989).

ROBERT SUTTER has specialized in Asian affairs with the Congressional Research Service of the Library of Congress since 1977. He currently is Chief of the Foreign Affairs and National Defense Division and a Senior Specialist in International Policy with the Congressional Research Service. He received a Ph.D. in history and East Asian languages from Harvard University, teaches regularly in Washington-area universities, and has published several books and articles dealing with contemporary China and Japan and their relations with the United States.

RAMON H. MYERS

Introduction:

A Unique Relationship

ON JANUARY 1, 1949, Chiang Ching-kuo accompanied his father, Chiang Kai-shek, to visit Dr. Sun Yat-sen's mausoleum and later to pray at a Christian church in Nanking.[1] In the previous two months, Communist armies had occupied Manchuria, consolidated their grip on North China, and mobilized for a massive assault to cross the Yangtze River and attack the Nanking-Shanghai area. Throughout 1949, opposition to Communist military forces melted away, and remnants of the government and armies of the Republic of China (ROC) made their way to Taiwan. On January 1, 1950, one year later, Chiang Kai-shek and his son were in Taipei. Chiang had decided to reform the Kuomintang (KMT) party and transform Taiwan into a model province to serve as a base for the eventual recovery of mainland China from Communist rule. Such was the dream that inspired the KMT's aging leaders.

Few at that time gave Chiang Kai-shek and the corrupt and inept Kuomintang any chance to succeed. Several years earlier, Theodore H. White and Annalee Jacoby had warned that "the greatest indictment of these men is their sheer inability to govern, to give leadership."[2] That assessment was shared by U.S. scholars, intellectuals, journalists and some policy makers. In fact, the Truman administration had abandoned Chiang's regime and would not have acted to defend Taiwan from the pending attack by Communist forces then being assembled across the Taiwan Strait.

U.S. policy abruptly changed when North Korean armored units advanced deep into South Korea on June 25, 1950. The U.S. government immediately moved its Seventh Fleet into the Taiwan Strait, preventing a Communist invasion, and reassessed its relationship with the beleaguered ROC government. Thereafter, the United States developed friendly relations with the ROC, recognized that government as representing China, and more important, extended economic and military aid to enable that island state to defend itself and launch economic development.

That friendship was sorely tested in 1978, when the United States established diplomatic relations with the People's Republic of China (PRC) and ceased to recognize the ROC as a nation-state. For the U.S. government, the ROC simply became Taiwan and its people. When Public Law 96-8 became law on April 10, 1979, the Taiwan Relations ACT (TRA) made possible a new relationship between the United States and the ROC—an informal relationship preserving existing laws and agreements so that trade, exchange of people, and the transfer of weapons and technology continued.

The connections between the ROC and the United States had been very special. From 1952 until 1968, the United States gave around $1.5 billion of economic aid, which did not include military assistance over the same period. Such assistance allowed the ROC to survive and build a modern economy with gradual democratization. To appreciate how the ROC benefitted from U.S. generosity, we ought to make clear the problems confronting the island state in the context of that state's bitter rivalry with the PRC.

Taiwan is an island comparable in size to the "combined area of Maryland and Delaware, or to Belgium, or to the Netherlands, but with much less arable land and far more people than any of them."[3] Spared a Communist invasion in 1950 because of the provident intervention of U.S. military power in the Taiwan Strait, the aging leaders of the ROC were determined to make a last stand on this tiny island and its offshore islets, the Pescadores, Matsu and Quemoy. Forty years later, Taiwan was unrecognizable to those who had lived there in 1950.

The Great Transformation

There was no reason that Taiwan should be the first society in Chinese history in which life chances for the Chinese people expanded, their living standards prospered, their personal freedom and liberty were guaranteed, and able leaders were increasingly selected by democratic means. In fact, the KMT's past history of failures should have dictated very different outcomes. But Taiwan's transformation was not only unique for a developing country after World War II but also was achieved without many of the human costs that have afflicted Western countries during their development of a century or more. By human costs, I refer to economic instability producing inflation and unemployment, economic growth with a worsening of income distribution, social divisiveness (such as conflicts between labor and management), social violence (such as urban crime), the spread of a drug culture, and other social pathologies affecting developed nations.

Moreover, the transformation of the ROC occurred in the face of severe obstacles. First, tensions and grievances had worsened between Taiwanese and mainlanders after World War II to produce the great February 1947 Uprising. Between February 28 and mid March, the Taiwanese seized control of the island's nine largest cities, only to be crushed by troops sent by the ROC government to suppress the Uprising. That Uprising spawned the Taiwanese Independence Movement, in which thousands of Taiwanese fled to Hong Kong, Japan, and the United States to organize an opposition party to topple KMT rule and establish an independent Republic of Taiwan. Memories of that Uprising remained strong among the Taiwanese in the 1950s and 1960s. A U.S. critic of the KMT regime remarked in 1970 that "despite the absence of violent domestic challenges to the Nationalist regime, rank-and-file Formosans have taken many risks to assure visiting diplomats and scholars of their political discontent."[4] Such discontent took the form of Taiwanese political apathy, the refusal of thousands of Taiwanese studying abroad to return after obtaining their advanced degrees, and constant Taiwanese criticisms of the Nationalist regime in private discussions with foreigners.

A second obstacle was rapid population growth and severe unemployment. Lacking natural resources, and depending on a few agricultural exports, the government decided to build new industries to reduce the imports of cement, steel, fertilizer, machine tools, and consumer goods, such as textiles. This drive for import substitution depended on enormous state subsidies, overvaluing Taiwan's currency, controlling foreign trade, and protecting industries from foreign competition. Although these protected industries indeed expanded production, few new jobs were created, domestic demand remained weak for goods from these developing industries, and their plants operated at high costs. By the 1950s, many officials questioned the import-substitution strategy and argued for more liberal policies that would promote export industry growth and end the privileges of importers, who were benefiting from the dual exchange rate system.[5]

A third major obstacle was the huge defense burden, which absorbed as much as 10 to 12 percent of the nation's gross domestic product in the first decade and nearly two-thirds of the state's annual budget. Supporting a defense force of close to a million people out of a population of around only nine or ten million in the 1950s produced severe social and economic strains.

Finally, the ROC somehow managed to avoid the many stresses that have paralyzed other developing countries and have made a transformation into modernity quite difficult. For example, intellectuals and students never organized and took to the streets and challenged the government, as in the Philippines, South Korea, and elsewhere. Trade unions never became powerful pressure groups demanding that wages rise more rapidly than productivity. New political parties never formed to sow confusion and challenge government policies. Finally, the ruling party never experienced serious factionalism to derail policy making and prevent the state from taking steps to deal with serious problems as they arose.

In the 1950s, the government promoted educational reforms to instill the Confucian values of harmony, compromise, and acceptance of moral authority, which helped to minimize conflict between students and teachers, labor and capital, and intellectuals and the government.[6] The economy grew at around 10 percent for nearly 40 years, and its three sectors—primary production (agriculture, forestry, fisheries), manufacturing, and services—were continually restructured. In the 1960s, a series of new economic policies were instituted to restructure the economy, enhance the island's export capability, and expand employment while raising productivity. With a growing gross domestic product, the government found it easier to shoulder a large defense burden and modernize the defense forces. Taiwan's population enjoyed high employment, low inflation, rising welfare and rapid urbanization.

By 1989, the successful government policies, the hard work and sacrifice of its citizens, and the close and friendly relations with the United States had produced a modernization miracle on Taiwan. The ROC boasted exchange reserves of over $75 billion and was the fifth-largest trading partner of the United States. Per capita income exceeded $6,000 per year. A highly urbanized society enjoyed great prosperity and tranquility. A highly educated citizenry had respect for the public weal. The largest number of foreign students in U.S. colleges and universities came from the ROC. Taiwan's cities still avoided the modern pathologies of a drug culture, serious urban crime, poverty of the elderly, and single-parent families. To be sure, urban crime was on the increase, and juvenile delinquency was of serious concern to authorities and parents alike, but social deviancy in Taiwan's densely populated urban centers paled in comparison with that in the cities of the West. Environmental problems had become serious, as elsewhere in the world, but government now spent more money to clean up environmental pollution.

In July 1987, the ROC leaders lifted martial law; in 1986, the press became free to print what it willed, and groups could demonstrate in the streets as long as they obeyed the rules. New political parties formed in 1986 and 1987, and the legislature and the judiciary increasingly challenged the government. Democracy had broken out in Taiwan. For the first time in Chinese history, a segment of Chinese society had achieved real economic and political modernization as experienced and understood in the West.[7] Paradoxically, a Confucian culture and an aging leadership defeated by the Chinese Communist Party had contributed to this great transformation.

Setting aside for a moment enlightened, able leadership, the good attributes of the Chinese, and the assistance rendered by the United States, was there not something else that contributed to this remarkable transformation? To be sure, both leaders and ordinary people believed that acquiring science and technology was good for society, that selecting leaders by a democratic process was desirable, and that having checks within government was necessary to correct the abuse of power. Yet, unless the leadership, the elite, and ordinary people shared some common ideas, merely valuing modern science and democracy might not be enough to nurture political and social integration and ensure economic development. It was these important values, shared by both the leaders and the people, that overcame the divisiveness of 1947 to produce a dynamic, urban, middle-class society based on Confucian ethics. These shared value orientations were consensus and pluralism.[8]

The consensus shared by many was the following. First, everyone seemed to endorse a capitalist economy based on competitiveness and private property. Second, everyone agreed that travel and contact with the outside world were extremely important and should be expanded whenever possible. Third, although society should be open to new ideas, Marxism should be rejected. Finally, Western liberalism should be embraced and connected with China's political and cultural heritage. Two important ideological systems merged to form this broad consensus—Confucianism and the doctrine of Sun Yat-sen, founding father of the ROC and the KMT.[9]

Confucianism provided the strong ethical foundations for strengthening the family and giving moral guidance and the impetus for individuals to develop according to their own will. One such shared ethical value was a deep respect for parental authority and the social authority of teachers and leaders. But Confucianism also emphasized self-fulfillment to become a highly moral person and to strive for knowledge and self-improvement. The educational reforms of the early 1950s greatly facilitated the spread of these values among the young.

Sunist thought, however, encouraged different shared orientations—a powerful respect for China as a nation-state striving for sovereignty and respect from other states, a sincere willingness to combine Western advances with China's rich heritage, and a desire to build a new China of great prosperity and democracy. Taiwan's officials believed in Sunist thought and were able to transcend disagreements and reach a consensus to support policies aimed at achieving equity with growth.[10]

A broad, well-educated middle class emerged that championed respect for and tolerance of diversity. New ideas, fashions, and lifestyles were promoted by this urban middle class. The proliferation of social networks of the urban middle class, including private associations, helped to speed the circulation of new ideas and foster diversity. As various groups championed new ideas in art, culture, business, and politics, pluralism gradually became a way of life in the ROC.

Consensus and pluralism characterize the value system that laid the foundation for progress in the ROC during the past four decades. As new attitudes and ideas became more widespread, the people continued to honor important traditions. What is astonishing is that this transformation took place within the context of a bitter rivalry between two Chinese states—in fact, a cold war version of the old civil war. That rivalry, in turn, was influenced by United States relations with both Chinese states.

Relations Between the Republic of China and the People's Republic of China Party (CCP)

The violent struggle between the Chinese Communist Party (CCP) and the Nationalist Party ended in 1949, but a contest between the PRC and the ROC still continues as to which system offers the best rewards to the Chinese people and can satisfy their centuries-long aspirations.[11] Beijing's leaders have made frequent overtures to Taipei's leaders to begin negotiations for unifying these two states under the formula of a single China with two different systems, *i-kuo liang-chih* (one country, two systems). But Taipei's leaders have rebuffed these overtures, instead offering their own solution: The ROC will make no compromise, have no contact, and make no agreements with the PRC until the system of Communist rule is radically reformed. By the late 1980s, however, many informal contacts were taking place. ROC business activities and investment had fostered a booming trade between Taiwan and mainland China, largely through Hong Kong. Taiwan's scholars and professionals were meeting their PRC counterparts in third countries. Citizens of the ROC were visiting their birthplaces in the PRC and spending large sums of money doing so. In fact, some PRC citizens began visiting their relatives in Taiwan.

Indeed, the Communist and KMT parties had established two fundamentally different systems that had moved along very different trajectories since 1950. The ROC's system had already been described. As for the PRC's political system, by 1956 Communist Party policies had destroyed all vestiges of a private market system based on private property and free contracting and had tried to replace the Confucian beliefs and values concerning family and kinship networks with socialist ethics emphasizing the primacy of the Communist Party, the glorification of the state, and the superiority of the collective form of life. Meanwhile, the Communist Party extended its control over the thought and behavior of all citizens. By 1957, widespread apathy and disillusionment with the new system had spread among the intellectuals, workers, and farmers. Supply shortages worsened. These new problems divided the Communist Party leadership. Competing ideas and rival leaders led to a violent power struggle over which vision and policies were most appropriate to bring China closer to socialism, or what party leaders might have called the *ta-t'ung* (Great Harmony).

In the 1950s, the party adopted a Soviet-style planned economy and social controls but then jettisoned these in the late 1950s and shifted to the radical ideas and organizations of Mao Tse-tung. Mao's mass movements based on class struggle were in turn cast aside in 1978 by Teng Hsiao-p'ing and his supporters, who then shifted to expanding contacts with the West and emphasized reform of the economy. By 1989, the Communist Party still adhered to Marxism and held absolute power to guide the country into socialism while insisting that only a proletarian dictatorship could keep the country on the proper road to socialism.[12] The party, however, has been persistently challenged from within and without to democratize and allow Western and Chinese ideas to compete with Marxism. Economic reforms have given the provinces greater power to use resources. As new tensions mounted in the 1980s, the party remained steadfastly committed to socialism, firmly believed that Marxism must serve China, and unswervingly maintained that only the Communist Party could achieve the socialist ideal for China.[13]

For four decades, then, the systems that governed each Chinese state evolved along opposite paths because of different doctrines, leadership styles, and organizations. Yet the Communist and Kuomintang parties have continually demanded that China be unified according to their respective doctrines and systems. I have referred to two Chinese states for two important reasons. First, both states have different constitutions and different forms of political governance that have evolved since the establishment of the ROC constitution in 1947 and the PRC's first constitution in 1954. As sovereign states, both conduct formal relations with other states and have different national flags and national anthems. Yet both continue to claim sovereignty over an entity called China. For these reasons, I will refer to these two different systems of governance as two sovereign Chinese states and make no pretense that the ROC does not exist, even though the U.S. government does not officially recognize the existence of the ROC government and instead only officially recognizes an entity its officials prefer to call Taiwan.

Given this historical reality, what have the leaders of these two Chinese states demanded? KMT leaders, such as Chiang Kai-shek, Chiang Ching-kuo, and his successor, Lee Teng-hui, have claimed that the KMT's historical mission is to have China unified under the governance of the ROC constitution and the doctrine of Sun Yat-sen. Not only did Chiang Kai-shek repeatedly describe that goal in his speeches and writings during his life spent on Taiwan, but his son also did the same. Writing on April 4, 1982, Chiang Ching-kuo remarked, "We shall raise our national flag on the mainland again and sing our national anthem together one day."[14] That hope was reaffirmed on July 8, 1988, when Lee Teng-hui, just elected chairman of the KMT, stated: "The Three Principles of the People are our guidelines. I sincerely hope that all members of the party will unite to work with one mind to find a new destiny for the nation and complete the historical mission of reunifying China under the Three Principles of the

People."[15] The ROC leaders have consistently stated their commitment to unify China under Sunist doctrine and the form of governance that now prevails on Taiwan.

The PRC leaders also have persistently asserted that their sacred mission is to liberate Taiwan and bring that island back to the motherland. On June 28, 1950, Chou En-lai declared that, "No matter what obstructionist action U.S. imperialists may take, the fact that Taiwan is part of China will remain unchanged forever."[16] For four decades, that position never changed. At the opening speech at the 12th National Congress of the Communist Party on September 1, 1982, Teng Hsiao-p'ing declared that the party's task in the 1980s was to "step up socialist modernization, to strive for China's reunification and particularly for the return of Taiwan to the Motherland . . ."[17]

Then, in mid 1984, Teng Hsiao-p'ing offered a new solution to the so-called Taiwan problem:

> What is the solution to this problem? Is it for socialism to swallow up Taiwan, or for the "Three Principles of the People" preached by Taiwan to swallow up the mainland? The answer is that neither can swallow up the other. If the problem cannot be solved peacefully, then it must be solved by force. This would do neither side any good. Reunification of the country is the aspiration of the whole nation. If it cannot be reunified in 100 years, then it will be reunified in 1,000 years. In my opinion, the only solution to this problem is to practice two systems in one country [*i-kuo liang-chih*].[18]

Under this new formula, Teng argued that Taiwan could retain its system, as Hong Kong will be allowed to do when British rule ends in 1997. Under this new arrangement, both Hong Kong and Taiwan would remain independent political entities but be part of China by virtue of direct trade and exchange of peoples. The PRC leadership no longer speaks of the liberation of Taiwan but of the necessity to have direct negotiations with the ROC leaders to establish the new "two systems in one country."

Teng has continually given assurances that "Taiwan can still practice capitalism while the mainland maintains socialism," an assurance he has made repeatedly for Hong Kong. The PRC leaders eagerly want to negotiate with the ROC leaders to set a timetable to establish the "two systems in one country" arrangement. In 1985, Teng further stated that the PRC would not station troops in Taiwan as it intended to do in Hong Kong. On September 16, 1985, the journal *Liaowang* announced that Taiwan would "be in charge of its own party, government and army" under the *i-kuo liang-chih* arrangement.[19] Since 1986, further statements have been made by Teng, Yang Shang-yun, and others elaborating on how the "two systems" might be created.[20] Frustrated by Taiwan's rebuff to these proposals, the PRC leaders frequently have stated that, if serious direct negotiations do not begin between the PRC and the ROC leaderships, the PRC might have to resort to force to initiate such discussions. That is where the matter now stands.

Behind the claims of both of these two Chinese states is an important shared assumption: Each state projects its sovereignty over the territory occupied and governed by the other. That shared assumption has shaped the foreign policies of both states. Neither Chinese government has agreed to have diplomatic relations with another state unless it renounces relations with the other Chinese government. Except in the case of international, intergovernmental organizations like the Asian Development Bank in the Philippines, the Olympics, and the International Council of Scientific Unions, where both states compromised and are members, neither state has agreed to participate in an international organization unless the other state has been removed. So strong, then, is the shared belief of each state's sovereign claim to the other's territory that neither state has retreated from its long-stated goal of eventually unifying China under its own doctrine and system of governance. To be sure, the PRC has proposed a compromise plan of setting up a "two systems in one country" arrangement, but this would be the prelude to the PRC eventually taking over the ROC.

The strong, passionate positions taken by these two Chinese states originated from two different ideologies—the Sunist doctrine of the KMT and Marxism-Leninism-Maoism of the CCP. The ideological convictions of both leaderships have not weakened since the early 1920s. Although new leaders have just begun to assume power in the late 1980s in both states, we can expect the KMT and CCP leaders in the near future (at least for a decade) to adhere to their different world views, claim sovereignty over the other, and insist upon the reunification of China under their respective doctrines and political systems. While publicly clinging to these different doctrines, both states are very likely to continue to expand their informal contacts until an eventual change in doctrine and foreign policy by one or both states takes place.

The role of the United States as a world power in Asia and the Pacific has been a fact of life that neither Chinese state could ignore except at its peril. The decision by the United States to continue to support the ROC after the Korean War broke out profoundly influenced the PRC leadership to choose isolation from the West and depend on the socialist bloc countries. Then, in 1978, when the United States chose to recognize the PRC, the ROC leadership insisted upon its principles and accepted international isolation. Only 24 countries in December 1988 continued to officially recognize the ROC, although the ROC still maintained semiofficial or nonofficial relations with 121 other countries.[21] Only by understanding the strong commitment to moral and ideological principles by these two Chinese states can we understand their conduct of foreign affairs.

The United States' China Policy in Historical Perspective

The United States' China policy, closely related to U.S. strategic concerns in the world, evolved through two phases after 1950. During the 1950s, the United States tried to contain the spread of communism on a global basis by establishing a balance of power in key geopolitical regions. United States political leaders perceived that the Soviet Union, in conjunction with allies like the PRC, promoted revolution in regions just decolonized from Western states' rule. Therefore, in Asia, the United States tried to isolate and contain the PRC's foreign policy through trade embargo and building alliances in the Pacific Basin. The U.S. State Department announced in May 1951 that the United States had no intention of recognizing the PRC and instead would recognize the ROC as having sovereignty over the mainland. Dean Rusk, then assistant secretary of state for Far Eastern affairs, explained the reasons for this policy on May 18, 1951, in a speech to the China Institute in New York:

> It is not my purpose, in these few moments this evening, to go into the specific elements of our own national policy in the present situation. But we can tell our friends in China that the United States will not acquiesce in the degradation which is being forced upon them. We do not recognize the authorities in Peiping for what they pretend to be. The Peiping regime may be a colonial Russian government—a Slavic-Manchukuo on a larger scale. It is not the Government of China. It does not pass the first test. It is not Chinese. It is not entitled to speak for China in the community of nations.[22]

United States policy makers contended that the PRC was only a client of the USSR and could not morally represent the Chinese people.

Public opinion in the United States was solidly behind this China policy, according to polls taken in the late 1950s.[23]

In the 1960s, the Sino-Soviet split and the great upheavals in China persuaded many U.S. legislators, journalists, intellectuals, and scholars to question U.S. China policy and suggest that at least the PRC should be recognized and seated in the United Nations (U.N.). Although U.S. leaders followed the China policy set in the 1950s, they began holding formal discussions with the PRC in third countries on such issues as freeing U.S. citizens held as captives in the PRC and the Vietnam war.

In the early 1970s, more flexibility characterized U.S. China policy. On April 14, 1971, President Nixon announced the lifting of the embargo on direct U.S. trade with China and relaxation of U.S. currency controls preventing the use of dollars by the PRC. On July 15, 1971, President Nixon announced that Chou En-lai had invited him to visit China "at an appropriate date before May 1972" and that he had accepted the invitation. President Nixon and Secretary of State Henry Kissinger conferred with PRC leaders in February 1972, which paved the way for agreements to increase trade and permit U.S. investments in China, such as the Kellogg Corporation's construction of fertilizer factories.

The new Nixon strategy called for détente with the Soviet Union and establishment of diplomatic relations with the PRC. This strategy assumed that the United States might help the PRC to become a counterweight to Soviet expansionism throughout the world. Tensions between the two communist giants had worsened when armed clashes broke out on Chan-pao (Damausky) Island in the Ussuri River on March 2, 1969, and again along the Amur River near Khabarovsk on July 8, 1969. But to placate the ROC, Nixon still hoped to have a "two China" solution, with each having membership in the U.N.[24] That hope dissolved in October 1971, when a U.S.-sponsored resolution in the U.N. not to expel the ROC lost by four votes, and a second resolution by Albania and 21 other countries calling for seating of the PRC was approved by 76 votes to 35, with 17 abstentions. Rather than trying to work with its friends in the U.N. to remain in that organization under a different arrangement, the ROC leadership decided to withdraw.

Although the United States continued to have security ties with the ROC and recognized the ROC as representing China, relations between the PRC and the United States rapidly improved. After Nixon and Kissinger met with Mao and Chou in Beijing, both sides produced the famous Shanghai communiqué on February 28, 1972.

The Chinese side declared that the PRC "is the sole legal government of China." Because Taiwan had once been part of "the motherland," liberating Taiwan was China's affair, and all U.S. forces must be withdrawn from Taiwan. By claiming sovereignty over Taiwan in this way, the PRC leaders merely adhered to long-standing principle. The United States acknowledged that the Chinese on both sides of the Taiwan Strait maintain that there is "but one China and that Taiwan is a part of China" and reaffirmed its interest in a "peaceful settlement" of the Taiwan issue by the Chinese people. Finally, the United States pledged eventually to withdraw military forces from Taiwan as long as "tension in the area diminishes." It was self-evident to Nixon and Kissinger when they conferred with Mao and Chou that these communist leaders preferred to set the issue of Taiwan aside in order to consider the larger issues related to PRC and U.S. security interests.[25]

Because the PRC leaders did not make an issue of Taiwan, PRC trade and cultural exchange with the United States rapidly advanced in the 1970s. President Carter decided in late 1978 to abrogate the U.S. security pact with the ROC and break diplomatic relations with the ROC. The status of Taiwan suddenly became unclear. At that moment, the U.S. Congress intervened and passed the Taiwan Relations Act (TRA). A unique relationship now began.

A Unique Relationship

Perhaps for the first time in the history of modern foreign affairs, a state had a broken relations with another, only to create a new legal arrangement so as to maintain virtually all the relationships that had existed before. The injured party even welcomed the new arrangement. How did this remarkable event come about, and how well has the new arrangement worked to the benefit of both states? In what way did the new arrangement reflect a new U.S. China policy, and what is that policy now? How well did the new arrangement protect the security of the ROC? How have the PRC and the ROC reacted to the new arrangement? What are the prospects for these two Chinese states to settle their differences and reach an agreement to coexist peacefully? Finally, what role might the United States be expected to play in the future? The five chapters that follow were written by five experts at a conference held at the Hoover Institution on September 10, 1988, and try to provide answers. They are briefly summarized below.

Ten Years of the Taiwan Relations Act

How was the United States to break relations with the ROC and still maintain trade and agreements? In 1979, both states had a two-way trade of $9 billion, U.S. investments in Taiwan totaled $666,192 million, some 60 treaties and mutual agreements existed, and their friendship had flourished for many decades. The Carter administration instructed the State Department in 1978 to draft legislation to handle these complex issues. Congress found this document unacceptable and instead held numerous hearings, which led to the drafting of Public Law 96-8, the TRA. This law defined *Taiwan* as meaning the people, their institutions, and "the governing authorities on Taiwan recognized by the United States as the Republic of China prior to January 1, 1979."[26] The TRA made it possible for the United States to have relationships with a territory that still claimed to represent China. All treaties and agreements formerly recognized by the two states would continue unless specifically terminated. The affairs of both states would be conducted through specially created unofficial offices in which all ROC affairs were accepted as the "undertakings of a foreign government."

The TRA began to function effectively and has remained in place ever since. Taiwan was treated as a state, and its government as a sovereign government, for all purposes of U.S. law. The United States operates the American Institute in Taiwan (AIT), which has its headquarters in Washington, D.C., and field offices in Taipei and in Kaohsiung. The ROC maintains the Coordination Council for North American Affairs (CCNAA) in Washington, D.C., with field offices in Boston, Houston, Chicago, Los Angeles, San Francisco, and five other cities. The respective offices interact with the official agencies of the ROC and the United States to handle all issues involving relationships between the two states.

All states, like married couples, eventually encounter difficulties, and the new U.S.-ROC relationship has been no exception. The first severe crisis erupted on October 15, 1984, when Henry Liu, a U.S. citizen of Chinese ancestry, was murdered in his garage in Daly City, California. Liu had just published a book critical of Chiang Kai-shek and his son Chiang Ching-kuo, who was then president of the ROC. Rumors circulated explaining the killing as an act of state terrorism concocted by the ROC government and undertaken by its paid agents to murder a citizen of the United States because that individual's behavior was judged dangerous to the national interests of the ROC. The Liu affair soon became politicized.

By December 1984, FBI investigators had briefed State Department officials, and officials at the highest levels of the AIT and CCNAA had exchanged information. By late January 1985, ROC officials had finished their investigations and arrested Admiral Wang Hsi-ling and his two deputies, Hu Yi-min and Ch'en Hu-men, for having instigated the assassination plot. A trial followed, and the ROC government invited U.S. observers to attend. Sentences were delivered, and the affair rapidly faded away. Both states had moved quickly to resolve the issue and prevent it from damaging their relationship. The cooperation offered by both states rapidly resolved the crisis, and justice seems to have been served.

As trade expanded, U.S. resentment about ROC markets remaining closed to U.S. businesses became more serious by the mid 1980s. High-level meetings between AIT and ROC officials have, so far successfully resolved these differences, and ROC markets have steadily become more open. However, the U.S.-ROC trade imbalance continues to grow, only showing some decline for the first time in 1988–1989.

In retrospect, the TRA machinery for conducting official relations between the United States and the ROC in the absence of normal diplomatic ties has worked remarkably well. The TRA has facilitated the expansion of trade and cultural exchange. More important, when serious difficulties between the two states arose, the TRA mechanism made it possible to find solutions.

Taiwan Relations Act and United States' China Policy

In the late 1970s, U.S. leaders and policy makers, fearful of a sustained Soviet military buildup and expanding Soviet influence in the Asian-Pacific region and elsewhere, believed that a strong PRC could serve U.S. interests by helping to check the Soviet Union in Asia and the Pacific. Such a view did not call for an explicit alliance between Beijing and Washington but only for the expansion of trade and cultural exchange between the two states and the sharing of information relevant to both countries' security. Therefore, there were strong concerns within the Carter administration when Congress decided to hold hearings about Taiwan and to draft a new law to preserve existing relationships with that country. Members of Congress were worried about Taiwan's security and wanted assurances that existing relationships could be preserved, even without diplomatic recognition.

Administration officials, however, feared that the new law might offend Beijing and pose difficulties for improving relations between the United States and the PRC.

After the TRA became law, a new crisis in U.S.-PRC relations arose when the Carter administration considered discussing the sale of advanced fighter aircraft to the ROC. The Carter administration refused to cooperate closely with Congress on this issue because officials believed that members of Congress might try to influence administration China policy, and the executive branch preferred conducting its China policy in secrecy without very much consultation with Congress. This fear originated from the long-standing disagreement between Congress and the executive branch as to how much power the executive branch should have to conduct foreign policy without congressional involvement. Rancor between the two branches began to spread once again.

The election of President Reagan gradually resolved the rift. During the first two years of his term, President Reagan decided not to sell more advanced jet fighters to the ROC, other than those already being provided, and the United States instead pledged to improve relations with the PRC. Congress perceived these developments to be the continuation of the Carter administration's China policy. By 1983–1984, however, the U.S. leadership began to downgrade China's strategic importance to the United States. This change came after George Shultz replaced Alexander Haig as secretary of state. The PRC now had severe economic problems, the United States had now developed a new military and political capability of dealing with the Soviet Union, and Japan and other Pacific Basin states were becoming far more important than China to the United States. Meanwhile, the PRC's leaders became aware that their political leverage over the United States had declined. Finally, the Reagan administration began to consult more closely with the ROC and to implement the TRA more vigorously, except for selling them new jet fighters. Under this new China policy, the important question was how the ROC could maintain its security under the TRA.

Helping the Republic of China To Defend Itself

The August 17, 1982 communique agreed to by the United States and the PRC marked a turning point for U.S.-ROC security relations. This public declaration pledged both the United States and the PRC to uphold previous agreements, such as the Shanghai communiqué and the terms for establishing diplomatic relations of January 1, 1979.

In particular, the U.S. government stated its intention that arms sales to the ROC would not exceed in quality and quantity the level of those supplied "in recent years since the establishment of diplomatic relations" and that the United States would gradually reduce its sales of weapons to the ROC, and eventually phase them out altogether. No mention was made by the United States, however, of how long the "long term" would be. There was also no mention of how slow the reduction of sales would be and what mix of weaponry would be sold each year. Certainly, nothing was mentioned about the supply of spare parts and allowing the ROC to contract with weapons producers in the United States on a private basis to acquire military technology. Finally, President Reagan interpreted this communiqué to be an agreement between the United States and the PRC that hinged on both Chinese states, especially the PRC, peacefully resolving their differences. In fact, the president made this remark:

> Regarding future U.S. arms sales to Taiwan, our policy, set forth clearly in the communiqué, is fully consistent with the Taiwan Relations Act. Arms sales will continue in accordance with the Act and with the full expectation that the approach of the Chinese government to the resolution of the Taiwan issue will continue to be peaceful. We attach great significance to the Chinese statement in the communique regarding China's "fundamental" policy, and it is clear from our statements that our future actions will be conducted with this peaceful policy fully in mind.[27]

The ambiguity of the communiqué and the abstract wording represented a new stage in U.S.-PRC diplomatic relations. This "gentlemen's agreement" allowed the United States to sell weapons to the ROC, but not improved weaponry. The PRC had extracted an important concession from the United States: The United States now promised to limit the quality and quantity of weaponry to be sold to the ROC. The PRC, however, had to accept the status quo relationship between the United States and the ROC because of the existence of the TRA. Yet, the security of the ROC was now in jeopardy. If the United States refused to supply the most advanced defensive weapons to the ROC, how could that state continue to upgrade its defense forces to maintain a balance of power with the PRC and deter the PRC from attacking the island? The ROC was in serious difficulty. Within a short time, possibly five years or so, the force deterrence possessed by the ROC might be insufficient to deter any PRC military attack. Unless the ROC acted promptly in 1983–1984 to upgrade its fighter airplanes, antinaval blockade capability, and antiamphibious forces, its security would be in great danger.

Recognizing this crisis, the ROC leadership decided to increase military expenditures to develop its own advanced fighter aircraft and other weapons necessary to deter PRC military aggression. The Reagan administration helped soften the harsh effect of the 1982 communiqué by reducing the value of arms sales each year slowly and making certain that the ROC received higher-quality weapons and equipment than it had before. The ROC now produces the defensive weapons that it cannot purchase from the United States. U.S. firms now provide technological assistance and even design and construction services. For any weapons on the U.S. munitions control or commodity control lists, U.S. firms must first obtain export licenses from the government. New major military production facilities are now located in the ROC.

By shifting to import substitution for obtaining advanced weapons systems, the ROC's security policy has changed the entire arms sale issue. If the United States remains willing to permit a military-related technology transfer to the ROC, and if the ROC government is willing to commit a major expenditure of human and budgetary resources to building a military-industrial complex, the ROC should be able gradually to enhance its capability to deter any PRC use of military force. That is where the matter now rests. But how did the PRC leadership view the enactment of the TRA and the cooperation between the United States and the ROC to maintain ROC security?

The People's Republic of China and the Taiwan Relations Act

The PRC leadership has always been committed to the goal of destroying the ROC regime and bringing the island of Taiwan and its people under its socialist system while using diplomatic negotiations with the United States to further these policies. We have already alluded to the negotiating tactics adopted by Mao and Chou when conferring with Nixon and Kissinger in 1971 in formulating the Shanghai communiqué. Both countries' leaders had then merely agreed to put the Taiwan issue on the back burner and to move forward on a step-by-step basis to achieve eventual diplomatic recognition. When the moment for normalization of relations came in 1978, the PRC then shifted tactics and demanded a complete rupture of U.S. relations with the ROC and the removal of all U.S. military forces from Taiwan.

The PRC leaders, however, were prepared neither for the response

of Congress and its drafting of the TRA nor for the Carter administration's acceptance of the TRA. The PRC leaders did not understand
this law and how its designers intended it to work, and they were
furious to finally learn that the TRA actually permitted the United
States and the ROC to have the same relationships as before but without diplomatic relations.

By not launching any campaign to pressure the United States immediately after the TRA became law, and by allowing nearly two
years to pass before vigorously responding, the PRC leaders lost their
opportunity to influence U.S. Taiwan policy. Even so, relations between the two countries slowly improved. By 1982, the PRC began to
stiffen its stand toward Washington and claimed that any arms sales to
the ROC violated the U.S. pledge to have only an unofficial relationship with Taiwan. Meanwhile, the PRC made a peaceful overture to
Taipei. On September 30, 1981, Yeh Chien-ying offered a nine-point
proposal calling for early negotiations between the CCP and the
KMT and promising the ROC leaders that Taiwan could enjoy a high
degree of independence as a special administrative region under the
PRC and even keep its armed forces, capitalist system, and way of life
as well as maintain relations with other foreign countries.

Yet the PRC continued to threaten the United States by hinting
that it might downgrade relations if the United States continued to
sell advanced weapons to the ROC. Tensions between the PRC and
the ROC were only resolved by the August 17, 1982 communiqué.
Beijing continued to express its displeasure with the TRA, but the
frequency and tone of these outbursts became muted and died in subsequent years. Beijing's leaders, however, never hesitate to publicly inform U.S. leaders at any opportune moment that the TRA intervenes
in the internal affairs of China and should be repealed and that the
United States is morally bound to eventually end all weapons sales to
the ROC. The PRC leaders realize that they cannot alter the TRA,
but they hope to initiate negotiations between Beijing and Taipei and
through direct relations manipulate events to enable the CCP to realize its long-held goal of the destruction of the KMT, the elimination
of the ROC, and the subjugation of Taiwan to PRC governance. Fully
understanding Beijing's intentions, how has the ROC viewed the
TRA?

The Republic of China and the Taiwan Relations Act

Keenly disappointed at Washington's decision to abrogate its security treaty and to break diplomatic ties, the ROC's leaders proposed

that the United States allow the ROC to continue to have trade and cultural exchange with the United States to maintain pre-existing treaties and agreements, to establish state-to-state mechanisms for facilitating exchange and communication, and to remain committed to preserving peace and prosperity in the Pacific Basin. These concerns were clearly communicated by the ROC to the United States, which positively responded, thus making it possible for the ROC to agree to a new arrangement that could substitute for normal diplomatic relations.

As weak a substitute as the TRA was for the 1954 security treaty and normal diplomatic ties, that law compelled the U.S. government to comply with all pre-existing treaties and laws between the United States and the ROC. Moreover, the TRA created a new organizational mechanism to substitute for the formal state embassy and consular machinery and still enable the two states to conduct all their affairs and resolve differences in a friendly and mutually satisfying way. Because both partners wanted this new arrangement, the TRA became law and has performed remarkably well during the past ten years to the satisfaction of both states.

A country's law is only as good as its enforcement. Will future administrations abide faithfully by the TRA? There is every reason to believe so.

It is clearly in the U.S. national interest to have peace and prosperity in the Pacific Basin, which means preserving the current status of the ROC and U.S.-ROC relations. The United States enjoys a prosperous trade with the ROC, which is its fifth-largest trading partner, and U.S. businesses, as of 1988, had invested $2.40 billion in that flourishing economy.[28] Taiwan is strategically located off the southeast China coast north of the important Soviet base in Vietnam. Under present international conditions, and with the KMT Party in charge, the ROC would definitely offer military basing rights to the United States if the Republic of the Philippines denied basing rights to the United States. This move could be made without negotiating a new security treaty. Finally, the ROC's successful economic modernization and rapid democratization offer a powerful challenge to socialist China to fundamentally reform its system. The ROC challenge might eventually force Beijing's leaders to undertake far-reaching, radical reforms of society, but that remains to be seen. For all these reasons, it is in the best interests of the United States that the TRA be vigorously enforced and the prosperity, peace, and stability of the ROC continue.

Conclusion

In mid 1988, "China fever" broke out in Taiwan with debate and discussion in the press about how the ROC could develop more contacts with the PRC, how the wealth of the ROC could be used to change the PRC's socialist system, and how the ROC would benefit if its businesses could invest and conduct business in the PRC. In 1988, the trade between Taiwan and mainland China, most of it through Hong Kong, had reached $2.4 billion, a 50 percent jump over the previous year. The great potential for more trade inspired many to criticize the government's "three no's" policy and call for a more flexible policy toward the PRC.

The PRC authorities were elated by this outbreak of "China fever" and welcomed the demands for more contact between the two states. Yet the PRC propaganda mill continued its steady barrage of radio broadcasts to Taiwan to pressure the ROC to negotiate directly with PRC leaders. On June 9, 1988, a commentator offered new incentives for Taiwanese businesses to receive special economic benefits if they would invest in the special zones on the mainland.[29] On July 5, 1988, another commentator lambasted the United States for intervening in China's internal affairs, blaming the "Taiwan problem" on the United States and complaining that the TRA had "placed Taiwan under U.S. protection and called for the United States to continue offering Taiwan the so-called defense service and to maintain a military balance in the Taiwan Strait.[30] On August 4, 1988, still another commentator accused the ROC government of trying to create "two China's in the international community."[31] These comments represent the diverse pressures that Beijing steadily has exerted on the ROC. Moreover, the PRC has never ruled out using force to get Taipei's leaders to negotiate. On June 14, 1988, Beijing announced that "China could not pledge never to use force to achieve reunification despite criticism from Taiwan.[32] These mixed signals combining threats with peaceful offers are constantly repeated.

In the past two years, 200,000 people from Taiwan already have had an opportunity to visit mainland China.[33] As these travelers describe their observations—a land of great backwardness, corruption, and overcrowding—many among the leadership, the elite, and the people doubt the benefits of reunifying two different systems. Many still insist that contacts take place only through third countries rather than directly. It is too early to predict how the evolving debate in Taiwan will be resolved about relations with the PRC.

Whatever the outcome, the United States is committed in principle to both Chinese states resolving their differences peacefully and has no intention of siding with one party to impose demands on the other.[34] This "two-point" policy, a core element of current U.S. China policy, is expected to remain in place. The TRA, therefore, offers the best hope for allowing sufficient time to elapse for further change to take place on both sides of the Taiwan Strait. After all, a decade has already passed with the TRA in place, and considerable change already has occurred within both of these two Chinese states.

The close U.S. ties with the ROC, made possible by the TRA, have nurtured more trade and cultural exchange between the two states, have enabled the ROC to provide for its security, and have found amicable resolutions to misunderstandings and difficulties. There is no reason why this "unique relationship" cannot persist well into the future.

Notes

1. Ching-kuo Chiang, *Calm in the Eye of a Storm* (Taipei: Li Ming Cultural Enterprise Co., 1978), p. 139.

2. Theodore H. White and Annalee Jacoby, *Thunder Out of China* (New York: William Sloane Associates, 1946), p. 311.

3. K. T. Li, *The Evolution of Policy Behind Taiwan's Development Success* (New Haven, Conn.: Yale University Press, 1988), p. 47.

4. Douglass Mendel, *The Politics of Formosan Nationalism* (Berkeley, Los Angeles: University of California Press, 1970), p. 111. Mendel's book probably contains the best collection of statements by Taiwanese expressing criticisms and moral outrage toward the Nationalist rule on Taiwan in the 1950s and 1960s. In particular, see chapter 5.

5. For some discussion of the negative consequences of this import substitution strategy pursued by the ROC government in the 1950s, see Ramon H. Myers, "The Economic Development of the Republic of China on Taiwan, 1965–1981," in Lawrence J. Lau (ed.), *Models of Development: A Comparative Study of Economic Growth in South Korea and Taiwan* (San Francisco, Calif.: Institute for Contemporary Studies, 1986), p. 15.

6. For a good review of how these moral principles were conveyed in the ROC education system, see Jeffrey E. Meyer, "Teaching Morality in Taiwan Schools: The Message of the Textbooks," *China Quarterly,* no. 114 (June 1988): 267–84.

7. See Ramon H. Myers, "Political Theory and Recent Political Developments in the Republic of China," *Asian Survey* 27, no. 9 (September 1987): 1003–1022.

8. I am indebted to Dr. Thomas A. Metzger for introducing me to these two concepts and discussing how they represented a new shared orientation among leaders, elite, and ordinary people in recent decades in the ROC.

9. For the best discussion of how these ideological orientations provided key norms to facilitate modernization on Taiwan, see Thomas A. Metzger, "Developmental Criteria and Indigenously Conceptualized Options: A Normative Approach to China's Modernization in Recent Times," *Issues & Studies* 23, no. 2 (February 1987): 19–81.

10. K. T. Li, *Taiwan's Development Success*, pp. 38–39, 75–76, 150–151, and 112–13.

11. Some of the argument in this section can be found in Ramon H. Myers, "The Contest Between Two Chinese States," *Asian Survey* 23, no. 4 (April 1983): 536–52.

12. For a discussion of these salient principles that currently shape the Communist Party line, see Ramon H. Myers, "Does the Chinese Communist Party Have a 'Line'?" *Issues and Studies* 23, no. 12 (December 1987): 120–38.

13. For a description of current conditions in the PRC and prospects for the next ten and twenty years, see Ramon H. Myers, "Mainland China's March Toward a New Socialism," in Annelise Anderson and Dennis L. Bark (eds.), *Thinking About America: The United States in the 1990s* (Stanford: Hoover Institution Press, 1988), pp. 63–88.

14. Ching-kuo Chiang, *Perspectives: Selected Statements of President Chiang Ching-kuo, 1978–1983* (Taipei: Government Information Office, 1984), p. 273. In fact, Chiang Ching-kuo repeatedly stated in the late years of his life that "together, we shall carry through the ideal of the 'unification of China under the Three Principles of the People' on a basis of our national spirit and ambition as expressed in loyalty and filial piety. In doing so, we shall console the souls of the ancestors of the Chinese people, our National Founding Father, the martyrs and of Father [Chiang Kai-shek] resting in Heaven." In this statement, one readily recognizes the Confucian spirit of that generation of leaders that guided the destiny of the ROC in the difficult decades after 1950.

15. *The China News*, July 8, 1988, p. 1.

16. Hungdah Chiu, ed., *China and the Question of Taiwan: Documents and Analysis* (New York: Praeger, 1973). Prior to Chou's statement, the United States had kept its ambassador to China in Nanking to explore the possibility of new relations between the communist regime and the United States, but the military invasion of South Korea by North Korea and U.S. reactions perhaps ended all hopes for any rapprochement between Beijing and Washington.

17. Communist Party of China, Central Committee, Bureau for the Compilation and Translation of Works of Marx, Engels, Lenin, and Stalin, *Selected Works of Deng Xiaoping* (Beijing: Foreign Languages Press, 1984), p. 396.

18. *Xinhua*, June 30, 1984, in *FBIS-China*, July 2, 1984, pp. E1–E2.

19. *Liaowang*, September 16, 1985, in *FBIS-China*, December 5, 1985, pp. U3–U5.

20. In particular, see the long statement by Yang presented in Los Angeles on May 26, 1987, insisting that Taiwan would enjoy a "high degree of autonomy" because the PRC would guarantee that it would not send personnel, troops, or staff to Taiwan. See *Xinhua,* September 6, 1986, in *FBIS-China,* September 8, 1986, p. B3.

21. *The China News,* July 9, 1988, p. 12.

22. Robert P. Newman, *Recognition of Communist China?* (New York: Macmillan, 1961), pp. 9–10.

23. Ibid., p. 15. As late as 1958, two out of three U.S. citizens polled expressed an unfavorable attitude toward the PRC.

24. Richard M. Nixon, *RN: The Memoirs of Richard Nixon* (New York: Grosset & Dunlap, 1978), p. 571.

25. Martin L. Lasseter, *U.S. Policy Toward China's Reunification* (Washington, D.C.: Heritage Foundation, 1988), p. 13.

26. Hungdah Chiu, ed., *China and the Taiwan Issue* (New York: Praeger Publishers, 1979), p. 267, Document 35, Taiwan Relations Act, 1979.

27. *Weekly Compilation of Presidential Documents, 1983* (Washington: Government Printing Office), pp. 1040–1.

28. Investment Commission, Ministry of Economic Affairs, *Chung-hua min-kuo li-mien heh-chun hua-ch'iao chi wai-kuo-ten t'ou-tzu, chi-shu ho-tso, tui wai-t'ou-tzu, tui wai-chi-shu ho-tso t'ung-chi nien-pao* [Annual Statistical Year Report of Overseas Chinese and Foreign Investment, Technical Cooperation, Outward Investment, and Outward Technical Cooperation in the Republic of China], December 31, 1988, p. 21.

29. *Daily Report: China,* FBIS-CHI-88-111 (June 9, 1988), p. 67.

30. *Daily Report: China,* FBIS-CHI-88-128 (July 5, 1988), p. 78.

31. *Daily Report: China,* FBIS-CHI-88-150 (August 4, 1988), p. 52.

32. *Daily Report: China,* FBIS-CHI-88-107 (June 3, 1988), p. 64.

33. *Daily Report: China,* FBIS-CHI-88-161 (August 19, 1988), p. 52.

34. Dennis Van Vranken Hickey, "America's Two-Point Policy and the Future of Taiwan," *Asian Survey* 28, no. 8 (August 1988): 881–96.

HARVEY FELDMAN

A New Kind
of Relationship:

Ten Years of the
Taiwan Relations Act

ON DECEMBER 15, 1978, President Jimmy Carter announced that two weeks later, at 12:01 A.M. on the first day of 1979, the United States would break diplomatic relations with the Republic of China on Taiwan (ROC) and would recognize the People's Republic of China (PRC) as the sole legitimate government of China.

Recognizing the government in Beijing as the government of China could not have been entirely unexpected. Although the United States considered the ROC de jure to be the legal government of China, since 1950 it had dealt with the PRC as the government in de facto control of the Chinese mainland. It had negotiated with the PRC at Panmunjom, at Geneva, and at Warsaw. After the PRC took China's seat in the United Nations (U.N.) in late October 1971, the United States necessarily consulted with it as a fellow permanent member of the Security Council. The Kissinger and Nixon visits to Beijing made plain that the trend of U.S. policy was toward eventual diplomatic recognition. Legislation passed by the U.S. Congress in 1973, regularizing the status of the PRC Liaison Office in Washington, took the process a step further by treating the PRC's officials stationed in the United States as diplomatic representatives with all the rights and immunities afforded by international law and custom. By the time of Carter's announcement, key members of Congress (both conservative and liberal), senior officials of three administrations, and two presidents, (Nixon and Ford) had visited Beijing, and all had treated their PRC hosts as the government of China.

But if recognizing the PRC de jure as the government of China was not a difficult step to take, breaking relations with the ROC certainly was. The United States was the ROC's most important trading partner, with two-way trade reaching $9 billion in 1978. Direct U.S. investment by that year had topped $500 million. Many leading U.S. corporations had factories on Taiwan. Roughly 5,000 U.S. civilians and twice as many U.S. military personnel and dependents lived on the island. The United States sold the ROC enriched uranium fuel for its nuclear power stations, a sale that U.S. law limited to "friendly governments." It was the ROC's major supplier of military equipment and defense services: $850 million worth of such items were contracted for in 1978. Some 60 treaties and executive agreements linked the two governments, including trade, investment and taxation treaties essential to orderly commerce, and a mutual defense treaty that made the ROC an ally of the United States. The United States had shouldered ultimate defense responsibility for the island ever since the Korean War broke out in June 1950. Many thousands of U.S. servicemen had been stationed on Taiwan over the years, and most had fond memories of their stay. In short, there was an interlacing of moral, political, economic, and strategic relationships more complex than the United States had with any other country—dating back to World War II with the alliance between Chiang Kai-shek and President Franklin Roosevelt—except for the U.S. relationships since the 1950s with Japan and the principal NATO allies.

The government in Beijing had insisted on three major conditions before agreeing to establish diplomatic relations: The United States must break diplomatic relations with the ROC, withdraw all U.S. forces from Taiwan, and end the mutual defense treaty. There were lesser conditions as well. The PRC wanted an end to all arms sales and took the view that all treaties and agreements concluded with the ROC were null and void and must lapse when relations were broken. The question of institutionalized contact after the U.S. embassy closed was particularly a key issue. During an August 1977 visit to Beijing, Secretary of State Cyrus Vance stated that the United States was prepared to recognize the PRC at an early date, but "it would be necessary for U.S. government personnel to remain on Taiwan under an informal arrangement." This was rejected by Teng Hsiao-p'ing, who described the proposal as reneging on promises made during the Ford administration that only an unofficial relationship "following the Japanese model" would continue.[1]

After reviewing the transcripts of Nixon, Kissinger, and Ford visits, senior Carter administration officials concluded that the promises made by the two previous administrations could not be withdrawn and that the "three conditions" would have to be accepted.[2] But even those most eager to establish relations with Beijing understood that the complexity of U.S.-ROC relationships and the strong sense of moral commitment felt by most U.S. citizens required a set of special arrangements. Thus, the United States would have to continue to sell arms so that the ROC could defend itself. As a great power, the United States could not simply abrogate the mutual defense treaty, as Beijing demanded. Instead, dignity required that it follow the procedure in Article 10 and give one year's notice of intent to withdraw. It would be necessary to continue to honor all the other treaties and agreements with the ROC in order not to upset trade and cultural relations. The unofficial office to be maintained after the embassy closed would have to be far more complex than that of Japan— in fact, would have to do everything that the embassy formerly did— and the entire relationship would have to be codified in a specific legislative act.[3]

The Taiwan Relations Act

Preliminary surveys about the kind of legislation that would be needed were made in the State Department in 1977– 1978, but the Carter administration considered the entire project so secret that more detailed study and legal drafting were not allowed until after the president's December 15, 1978 announcement. At that point, teams of lawyers in the State Department were hastily convened, and they, consulting with colleagues in the Departments of Justice, Commerce, and Treasury, the Export–Import Bank, the Nuclear Regulatory Commission, and elsewhere in government, hurriedly produced a draft bill, which the administration then passed to the Congress.

The proposed legislation, drafted in the State Department and handed to the foreign affairs committees of House and Senate, was purely technical. It dealt with such matters as the applicability of laws; the creation, staffing, and functioning of the American Institute in Taiwan (AIT), which was to take the place of the former U.S. embassy; and operations of the Overseas Private Investment Corporation. It referred repeatedly to "the people on Taiwan," a phrase imposed by policy makers in the State Department that, though never defined, was intended to refer to the government of the ROC and its people in a way that would not offend the PRC. The phrase "people of Taiwan" (instead of "on Taiwan") was specifically rejected as implying that Taiwan was a separate state.

The law enacted by Congress was quite different. Irate at not having been consulted by the Carter administration on a matter as important as recognizing Beijing and breaking relations with the ROC—a consultation specifically requested by an amendment to that year's International Security Assistance Act[4]—the Congress accepted the technical portions of the administration draft but wrapped them in an entirely new political context that spelled out unambiguously the congressional view that strong political, security, and economic ties must continue to link the ROC and the United States.

Public Law 96-8, the Taiwan Relations Act (TRA), begins with a six-point statement that it is U.S. policy

1. To preserve and promote extensive, close, and friendly commercial, cultural, and other relations between the people of the United States and the people on Taiwan

2. To regard peace and stability in the area as in the political, security, and economic interest of the United States, and as matters of international concern

3. That the establishment of diplomatic relations with Beijing rests on the expectation that the future of the ROC will be determined solely by peaceful means

4. That any attempt to determine that future by other than peaceful means, including use of boycott or embargo, would be regarded as a threat to the peace and security of the Western Pacific and a matter of grave concern to the United States

5. To continue to provide defensive arms to the ROC, but without consultation with the PRC

6. To maintain a capacity to resist any form of coercion exerted against the security or social or economic system of the ROC.

In a key departure from administration wishes, the Act makes it a matter of law that the United States "will make available to Taiwan such defense articles and defense services as may be necessary to enable Taiwan to maintain a sufficient self-defense capability" and that, in deciding what weapons are necessary, the president and Congress are to consider only the ROC's needs and not PRC wishes.

Senators Glenn and Javits added another very important provision:

"The president is directed to inform the Congress promptly of any threat to the security or social or economic system of the people on Taiwan, and any danger to the interests of the United States arising therefrom. The president and the Congress shall determine, in accordance with constitutional processes, appropriate action by the United States in response to any such danger." As the Senate report on the bill pointed out, this language makes the law into something very close to the mutual defense treaty with the ROC, which the administration had given notice of intent to terminate on December 31, 1978. The House report added: "If, nonetheless, an armed attack or use of force were to occur, the legislation makes clear there should be a prompt response by the United States. What action would be appropriate, including possible use of force in Taiwan's defense, would depend on the specific circumstances."

Finally, the law defined "Taiwan" as meaning the people, their institutions, and "the governing authorities on Taiwan recognized by the United States as the Republic of China prior to January 1, 1979."[5]

The congressional committees that drafted the TRA did accept the more technical features of the administration draft, such as those dealing with the American Institute on Taiwan, applicability of laws, eligibility for Export–Import Bank support, and Overseas Private Investment Council guarantees. In doing so, they paid their only compliment to the administration. The report of the Senate Foreign Relations Committee stated: "The bill submitted by the administration takes no position on the status of Taiwan under international law, but does regard Taiwan as a country for purposes of domestic law. The bill assumed that any benefits to be conferred on Taiwan by statute may be conferred without regard to Taiwan's international legal identity. The legal scholars consulted by the Committee agreed with this view."[6]

The TRA was a unique solution to a unique set of problems. For the first time in its history, the United States was breaking relations with a friend, an ally, and one of its most important trading partners. It was doing so not because of any dispute between the two governments, and certainly not because of any provocation from the ROC. The break stemmed solely from a political situation in which the government in Taipei claimed to be the legal government of all of China, despite the unmistakable fact that for almost 30 years the government in Beijing had ruled China. Even after the Nixon visit in 1972 and the issuance of the Shanghai communique, had the ROC sought U.S. recognition as something other than the legal government of all China, there would have been intense political pressure in the United States to grant such recognition, despite the consequences for relations with the PRC. But by sparing themselves the intensely complicated constitutional questions such a step would raise, the authorities in Taipei made it inevitable that one day recognition would be transferred to Beijing.

Now that day had come, and the TRA was passed as the charter of a wholly new and unprecedented relationship, in which a government no longer formally recognized nevertheless would continue to be treated as such, not only for all domestic concerns but also for many international concerns as well. In order to continue providing enriched uranium for nuclear power reactors, the United States was to consider the ROC a "friendly government." Although the PRC was recognized as the legal government of China, nevertheless, as a matter of law, this recognition would have no effect on property in the United States held by the ROC as the government of China. For purposes of the U.S. Immigration and Nationality Act, the ROC would continue to be treated as a country separate from China. Immunities granted under the Foreign Sovereign Immunities Act would continue. Acts of the Coordination Council for North American Affairs, the ROC's unofficial instrumentality in the United States, were to be accepted as the undertakings of a foreign government. And all treaties and agreements between the United States and a government no longer recognized as a government were to continue indefinitely unless specifically terminated.

All treaties, that is, except the mutual defense treaty, which was to run just one year longer. The United States followed the procedure specified in Article 10 and gave twelve months' notice of intent to withdraw. But during that year, from January through December 1979, the United States would continue to have a specific treaty obligation to defend a derecognized ROC against attack from the government the United States had just recognized. Even after the treaty ended, the United States would continue to have expressed in its laws a commitment to the security of the ROC and its people, and successive presidents would have a legal obligation to consult with Congress on measures for its defense, were Taiwan to be attacked.

Never before in history had there been such a piece of legislation.

Senior officials of the Carter administration, including the president, were deeply troubled by the bill as it emerged from Congress. The PRC press and its representatives in Washington had been most vitriolic in attacking the legislation as it moved through the House and Senate. Some senior officials in the State Department and the National Security Council staff urged the president to veto the bill on the grounds that it constituted a new defense treaty with the ROC and thus laid the administration open to the charge of having negotiated in bad faith with Beijing. The PRC, these officials said, would never accept the Act, and thus relations would be damaged at their very onset.

But others doubted that damage would be so real or so lasting. They pointed out that Beijing at the time was heavily engaged in hostilities with Vietnam in which its armed forces were not doing well and that the U.S. connection was bound to be valued, if only for psychological reasons vis-a-vis Hanoi and Moscow. They pointed to the many U.S. interests at stake and the imperatives of more than $9 billion in trade and half a billion dollars in investments. The U.S. relationship with the ROC was too complex not to have a legal basis and too important to too many people to leave untended for long. Reluctantly, the president signed the bill.[7]

Negotiating a Modus Vivendi

The passage and signing of the TRA made Beijing angry and Washington uneasy, and the mood in Taipei was volatile, to say the least, and had been so since Carter's recognition announcement. Despite the statements of three U.S. administrations that normalization of relations with the PRC was inevitable, and despite Carter's own assertion soon after taking office that he had made normalization a goal for his first term as president, the ROC and its people reacted to the December 15 announcement with shock, outrage, and a degree of panic. Shortly thereafter, the car carrying Deputy Secretary of State Warren Christopher, who had come to Taiwan to open negotiations on how relationships might continue on an unofficial basis, was attacked by a mob, its windows smashed, and the deputy secretary spat upon. In Washington, some ROC representatives worked hard to stir up anti-Carter protests across the country, and one was declared persona non grata as a result. (Interestingly, on some college campuses, extreme Maoist groups also protested the administration action, claiming that U.S. recognition of the "bourgeois revisionist" government in Beijing headed by Teng Hsiao-p'ing was a "crime against the Chinese people.")[8] In general, the initial ROC attitudes were refusal to accept that the United States in fact had recognized its adversary in Beijing as the government of China and an intense desire to find some way of turning the clock back.

Carter administration officials were angered by ROC behavior, especially by the attack on Deputy Secretary Christopher in Taipei, and some made a point of reacting harshly to later ROC requests. Nevertheless, it was necessary for the two sides to find a mutually agreeable way of conducting business in the absence of normal diplomatic ties. Accordingly, with Ambassador James Shen soon to depart from Taipei, Vice-Minister of Foreign Affairs Yang Hsi-k'un was sent from Taipei to negotiate on behalf of the ROC. His principal U.S. interlocutor was Deputy Assistant Secretary of State Roger W. Sullivan, who had been with Christopher when the attack on his car took place. Certain legal questions were discussed separately by a team of lawyers from Taipei and Senior Deputy Legal Adviser Lee Marks for the United States. The author also represented the United States and took notes for the United States at all discussions.[9]

The negotiations began at the end of December and were not concluded until February. They thus proceeded simultaneously with congressional consideration of the TRA. This gave a bizarre quality to some of the negotiations, for certain points that Yang could not get Sullivan to concede (for example, no diminution in the number of offices that the ROC would be able to have in the United States and diplomatic privileges for its representatives) were reported to the ROC's friends in Congress, who then wrote them into the TRA.

At the outset, Yang and the ROC negotiators pressed hard for continuation of relations in some official form. Told that liaison offices on the former U.S.-PRC model could not be accepted and that a modified "Japanese formula" was the best that could be offered, Yang continued to insist that the relationship with the United States must be described as having "qualities of officiality" in order to be acceptable to his government and people. He further insisted that the instrumentality to be set up by the ROC would have to be an official one if it were to operate effectively.

Weeks of argument ensued. Ultimately, the ROC dropped its insistence on official representation when it became clear that Congress would not support them on this issue by writing it into the TRA. An additional factor was the administration's point that unofficial representatives could have access to senior policy makers within the executive branch, but official representatives would have to be refused that access. However, the Carter administration later reneged on its promise that unofficial representatives from the ROC could call on U.S. officials in their offices. Instead, it insisted that these contacts must take place outside official premises of the executive branch. This precedent was largely followed by the Reagan administration as well.

In general, the United States tried to keep the focus on practical arrangements for continuation of necessary and desirable relationships. The ROC felt reassured that the agreement would deal effectively with substantive matters from visas to bank deposits but nevertheless considered the form of the new relationship to be equally important. The "qualities of officiality" issue was settled finally by the author's suggestion that the United States must describe the new relationship as entirely unofficial but had no way of preventing the ROC from describing it otherwise.

One of the last points to be settled was the name of the ROC's new instrumentality. After being informed that the United States proposed to call its office the American Institute in Taiwan (AIT), the ROC wished to create a parallel "ROC Institute in America." The United States rejected the idea of any office with the name *China, Chinese, Republic of China,* or *ROC.* Even use of the term *Taiwan* would present problems for the United States since it would imply acceptance of a "one China, one Taiwan" position. Asked informally what name would be acceptable when so many had been ruled out, the author pointed out that the division in the Ministry of Foreign Affairs with responsibility for relations with the United States was called the North American Affairs Bureau. He suggested, also quite informally, that the ROC consider using some variation on that name, such as Institute or Council for North American Affairs. The suggestion was accepted, and the Coordination Council for North American Affairs (CCNAA) was born.

The TRA was passed by the House of Representatives on March 28 and by the Senate on March 29, 1979, and was signed into law by President Carter on April 10, 1979. Executive Order 12143 on June 22, 1979, made the necessary changes in the United States code. It remained to be seen how the new relationship would work in practice.

The Taiwan Relations Act
in Operation

The political heart of the TRA lies in the statements of political policy in Section 2 and the security guarantees contained in Section 3, but the practical genius of the act is to be found in Section 4, on the application of laws, and in the Sections from 7 onward that deal with the AIT and the parallel ROC instrumentality, the CCNAA. Important as the policy statements were for reassuring the ROC and for restraining any PRC tendency toward adventurism, it is Section 4—which states that Taiwan shall be treated as a state and its

government shall be treated as a sovereign government for all purposes of U.S. law—that provided a stable base for the new relationship. Similarly, the successful operation of the two unofficial
instrumentalities created the functional equivalent of close diplomatic
ties and sustained relations between the United States and the ROC
that otherwise might have attenuated or even disappeared.

The AIT has its headquarters in Washington, D.C., and field offices in Taipei and Kaohsiung. It is incorporated in the District of Columbia as a nonprofit institution, ostensibly governed, according to its
bylaws, by a board of directors appointed by the secretary of state,
but in fact it takes policy direction from the State Department's Bureau of East Asian and Pacific Affairs. The secretary of state also ap-
points the heads of the Washington and Taipei offices, and the institute
is funded as a line item in the State Department budget. It is staffed by
government officials, most of them from the Foreign Service but including officers from Defense, Commerce, and other agencies as well,
all of whom are technically placed on leave status during the period of
their service with AIT. Nevertheless, their AIT service counts toward
retirement and promotion credit, their medical insurance and other
government benefits continue uninterrupted, and their pay continues
at the level of their former government position. Although they technically are not consular officers, the Act authorizes them to perform
services to U.S. citizens on Taiwan as though they were. AIT's offices
in Taipei and Kaohsiung are regularly inspected by the Foreign Service
Inspection Corps of the State Department, and these inspectors rec-
ommend changes in AIT operations and audit its finances.

There have been four directors of AIT's Taipei office since the
TRA was passed. All have been senior government officials, and two
were former ambassadors. Charles Cross, the first director (1979–
1982), had been ambassador to Singapore and had a connection with
China policy going back to the 1950s. He tended to take a rather low
profile and did not particularly seek contact with ROC officials, as
was in keeping with the office's new status. His successor, James Lilley
(1982–1984), later the U.S. ambassador to the Republic of Korea, had
a far more outgoing personality, and, although still careful not to become a public figure in Taipei, he steadily expanded the office's range
of contacts to include senior Taiwanese political figures. Harry E. T.
Thayer, another former ambassador to Singapore, adopted a lower
profile, and during his tenure (1984–1986) AIT again faded from public notice. David Dean, the current director in Taipei, was the first
director of AIT in Washington following normalization, and therefore
he is more fully aware than any of his predecessors of the evolution of

the institution, its methods of operation, and the history of the problems AIT must deal with. Long a familiar figure among ROC economic and political decision makers from his prior service in the U.S. embassy in Taipei as well as from his association with AIT since its establishment, Dean enjoys broad contacts in both capitals and is highly regarded.

Despite differences in personality and public visibility, all the directors of AIT Taipei have been able to secure appropriate access to senior figures in the ROC government whenever necessary. They interact on the ministerial level with ROC officials, and the ROC presidential office has been open to them. AIT Taipei negotiates when required, reports and analyzes political and economic trends, monitors end use of arms sold to the ROC, assists U.S. exporters, promotes trade and tries to settle trade disputes, operates a cultural exchange program and a library, provides consular services to U.S. citizens on Taiwan, and processes visas for ROC citizens through a special arrangement with the U.S. Consulate General in Hong Kong (the formal issuer of the visas). In short, it does just about everything that the U.S. embassy in Taipei did in the past. The AIT branch in Kaohsiung bears a relationship to the Taipei office that is analogous to that of an outlying consulate to its embassy.

In 1987, 110,000 ROC citizens applied to AIT for nonimmigrant visas to the United States (that is, visas to visit temporarily as tourists, businessmen, or students). Ninety thousand of these applicants were issued visas. Applicants are interviewed by AIT officers, and the information is sent electronically to Hong Kong, which authorizes issuance of the visas, usually within 24 hours. In addition, approximately 10,000 immigrant visas were issued in 1987 to ROC nationals, but for these a trip to Hong Kong (or to another consular office abroad) is required because the law mandates a personal interview with consular officers in such cases. Some 850 passport applications from U.S. citizens in Taiwan were received in 1987. All these applications are taken by AIT officers in Taipei, and the data are then transmitted to Hong Kong, which issues the passport (usually within two weeks) and mails it back to Taipei.[10]

About the only consular functions not performed at AIT Taipei are shipping and seaman services. Here the law provides very strictly that seamen can be signed on or off a U.S. registered ship only by a U.S. consular officer. But AIT officers register births and deaths, provide notary services, send witnesses to the rare trials of U.S. citizens in the ROC, and visit those few U.S. citizens in prison. ROC officials routinely notify AIT when a U.S. citizen is arrested and provide the equivalent of consular access. During their inspection of AIT Taipei in 1987, Foreign Service inspectors recommended that immigrant visas and passports be physically issued there, but this recommendation has not been accepted by the State Department. The consular section at AIT Taipei is staffed by fourteen Americans, including three who work part-time, and by 37 ROC nationals. This makes it one of the largest U.S. consular operations abroad.

At first, it was quite difficult to get government officers to resign from their various services, even temporarily, to take assignments with the AIT in Taiwan. That is not the case now, and AIT Taipei and Kaohsiung are regarded as plum assignments. Housing and schools are good, the people are friendly, and there is no terrorism problem. Aside from these personal considerations, professional ones are positive as well. AIT gives more responsibility to junior and mid-level officers than they are likely to get at a normal foreign service post, which makes for greater job satisfaction and career advancement. The current head of the economic affairs section at AIT Taipei has just been named consul general in Sydney, which is considered to be one of the best assignments the foreign service can bestow.[11]

The offices of the CCNAA in the United States operate in similar fashion, but with two significant differences. Since the United States and not the ROC insists on the fig leaf of unofficiality, the CCNAA relationship with its Ministry of Foreign Affairs is even closer and more open than the State Department-AIT relationship. CCNAA issues visas and performs consular services in its own name. Second, in the pattern established since the TRA was passed, most negotiations between the two governments take place in Washington rather than in Taipei. Therefore, the chief ROC representative in Washington (called the representative) and his senior staff must have even more frequent contact with policy-making leaders in the executive branch and with congressional leaders than his U.S. counterpart in AIT Taipei. When the CCNAA director in Washington has been as able and vigorous as Dr. Frederick F. Chien, now replaced by Dr. Ting Mo-shih, the current chief representative, this kind of access gives him a degree of influence on host country decision makers that no AIT director has ever enjoyed. Indeed, few ambassadors accredited to the United States have had Dr. Chien's access and influence.

By agreement between the two governments, both CCNAA and AIT enjoy secure communications. AIT officers in the ROC, like CCNAA officers in the United States, have duty-free entry privileges for household effects but not for other items. Both enjoy what is called functional immunity—that is, they cannot be arrested or tried for acts committed in the line of duty. In theory, CCNAA staff in the United States and AIT staff in the ROC could be prosecuted for committing criminal acts unconnected with their work, but unless the matter were particularly serious the offender more likely would be expelled. In any case, such a situation has not arisen.

The substitution of the AIT-CCNAA mechanism for embassies and consulates has not diminished interaction between the two governments. Some 30 new agreements have been negotiated since the breaking of diplomatic relations, most of them signed in Washington between the AIT and CCNAA. Ostensibly, these are "private" agreements between the two instrumentalities. Actually, they are the equivalent of executive agreements between the two governments covering such matters as civil aviation, scientific interchange, electronic communications, and cooperation in oceanographic research, issues not normally within the compass of private institutions.[12]

From Washington, interaction flows through AIT as a facilitator, not as a policy-making body. At the beginning of the new relationship, Carter administration officials insisted that information flow through AIT and that AIT act on behalf of the United States in reality as well as in theory. This quickly proved impractical. AIT simply is not large enough to substitute for the myriad agencies of the U.S. government, and it cannot be expected to acquire expertise on the entire range of governmental concerns from atomic energy to agricultural price supports. Quickly a pattern was established that necessary action would be taken by the relevant government agencies themselves and communicated by AIT to CCNAA.

Also as part of the initial pattern, all meetings between CCNAA and U.S. government officials had to take place either at AIT offices or in neutral territory, such as in restaurants. But the ROC is now the United States' fifth-largest trading partner, and the United States is the ROC's largest trading partner, so trade, commercial, and military relationships are too complex to be handled in this way. AIT officials simply could not eat so many meals, and their budget would not allow such frequent resort to restaurants. The current practice is that CCNAA officials are free to call on their U.S. government counterparts in their offices so that the business of the two governments can be more efficiently accomplished. The only exceptions to this rule are the State Department and the Executive Office of the President (which includes the Office of Management and Budget, the National Security Office, and other White House staffs).

To demonstrate how the staffs work, let us take the theoretical example of a request from an ROC ministry for information regarding certain U.S. labor practices. A junior or mid-level CCNAA officer will call at the appropriate office in the U.S. Department of Labor and make the necessary request. The matter is too complex for the information to be communicated then, so he is told to make the request by letter. He will address the letter to AIT and send the original there, not to the Department of Labor, but he will send a copy of the letter directly to the official at Labor with whom he discussed the matter. That official will prepare a reply and send it to AIT. It will then be sent to CCNAA as an AIT response. The procedure is cumbersome, but it works. The general rule is, when a written record is to be created, it will be created by AIT.

The more senior CCNAA officials, including the director and his deputy, face more stringent rules. Their meetings with senior executive-branch officials still take place either at AIT headquarters or in restaurants. This has been something of an obstacle to efficient operation at times when trade and financial problems have been serious and persistent. Trade problems, for example, probably could be handled more smoothly if the CCNAA director were allowed to call on the president's special trade representative or his deputies in their offices instead of requiring the two sides to meet at AIT's Washington headquarters or negotiate over restaurant meals.[13]

The Congress applies no similar restrictions, however, and high-level office calls do take place there. Similarly, members of the ROC National Assembly and the Legislative Yuan, including members of both the Kuomintang and the Democratic Progressive Party, are allowed to call on State Department officials in their offices.

CCNAA headquarters in Taipei operates on a far smaller day-to-day basis than AIT Washington. In Taipei, the polite fiction that all matters are handled between AIT and CCNAA is not pursued in a consistent way, and the government objects to direct contact between its officials and AIT Taipei only when it wishes to make a point to the U.S. government about reciprocity.

The April 1988 trade talks between the United States and the ROC provide a good example of how matters are handled in Taipei. These negotiations are an annual event, sometimes held in Taipei and sometimes in Washington. In April 1988, they were initiated by a letter from AIT Taipei to CCNAA headquarters in Taipei. Once the talks were agreed to, a team made up of officials from the Office of the Special Trade Representative and the Departments of Commerce, State, and the Treasury came to Taipei. The delegations were nominally headed by the senior economic officer of AIT Taipei and his opposite number in CCNAA Taipei, but after the formal opening plenary session the meeting split into committees made up of experts on each side to deal with the several matters at issue—such as intellectual property rights and the ROC's barriers to certain U.S. agricultural exports. Within these committees, of necessity government experts talk directly to government experts. If the AIT and CCNAA officials have substantive knowledge of the issues, they play an active role in the talks. But if they do not, the mechanism has evolved to the point where the United States no longer insists on the cover of AIT-to-CCNAA mediation. In matters as important as these, involving literally billions of dollars in trade, there can be little room for the polite fiction that these are not government-to-government negotiations.[14]

As officials now serving at CCNAA Washington see it, their operations can be divided in three phases, corresponding to the three directors who have headed that office. Konsin Shah was CCNAA's first Washington director, taking over from Vice-Minister Yang Hsi-k'un after the conclusion of negotiations in 1979. This was a time of great uncertainty, with both sides feeling their way into the new relationship. Most CCNAA officers were former staff of the just-closed embassy, and much of their time was taken up with adjusting to having to live and work in totally new and unaccustomed ways. They had to move out of the embassy building and find new offices. Diplomatic license plates for their vehicles had to be returned, and the cars reregistered. In some cases, new visa status was necessary. All of this took time and energy in a period when most were still shocked at the break in relations. Under these circumstances, it was hard to work effectively.

By the time the second director, Dr. Ts'ai Wei-p'ing, took over, the new method of operation had become more institutionalized, and the emotional pain stemming from the break in relations had lessened. The ROC expected much from the new Reagan administration, particularly since the president, during his campaign for the Republican nomination, had spoken of reconstituting an official U.S.-ROC relationship. These hopes were disappointed, however, when the new administration's actions failed to match its rhetoric. At the same time, Dr. Ts'ai was advanced in years, and neither he nor his senior deputies were in good health. CCNAA was unable either to pursue vigorously those opportunities that the change in administrations might have afforded or to keep the United States from moving closer to the PRC. The ROC suffered a particular blow when the Reagan administration—ostensibly the friendliest the ROC could hope for—in the joint communique of August 17, 1982 agreed to cut back arms sales to the

ROC, despite the fact that such an undertaking was contrary to the clear language of the TRA.

The ROC's third director, Dr. Frederick F. Chien, was a far more able diplomat than his two predecessors and was also younger and more vigorous. Having concentrated on relations with the United States for most of his career, he understood U.S. political and economic realities quite well and had many contacts among key figures. Under his leadership, CCNAA's activities and influence—particularly its influence with the Congress—expanded enormously.

It was fortunate for the ROC that Chien and his senior deputies were in Washington at this particular time because political, commercial, and financial problems threatened the reconstructed relationship with the United States. On the political front, a new organization of ethnic Taiwanese in the United States, the Formosa Association for Public Affairs, was gaining prominence and enlisting congressional allies in attacks on ROC human rights policy. Meanwhile, the enormously expanding volume of trade and the rapidly growing U.S. trade deficit brought many problems requiring expert handling and negotiation. Putting the relationship back on an even keel required hard and sustained work by Chien and his associates and difficult decisions at the highest levels of government in Taipei.

The Liu Case as an Example of Crisis Management

Henry Liu, a U.S. citizen of Chinese ancestry who also used the pen name Chiang Nan, was murdered in the garage of his home in Daly City, California, on October 15, 1984. Liu had written a book about Chiang Ching-kuo, then ROC president, which contained material about Chiang's private life that some on Taiwan considered scandalous. It also included blunt criticism of his actions as de facto ruler after his father, President Chiang Kai-shek, became incapable of governing about 1972. According to Liu's wife, in 1977 Admiral Wang Hsi-ling, then the ROC naval attache in Washington, warned Mr. Liu not to write about the Chiang family. In 1984, Wang was director of the Ministry of Defense Intelligence Bureau.

At the time Liu was killed, he was working on another book, this time about Wu Kuo-chen, a former governor of Taiwan, and apparently this book would also contain some fairly lurid gossip about the Chiang family. Shortly before Liu's death, according to Mrs. Liu, Henry Liu had signed an agreement with the Wu family that would give him access to Wu Kuo-chen's personal papers and archives.

Liu's murder was quickly perceived as a political assassination.

The Daly City police brought the Federal Bureau of Investigation (FBI) into the case. Within weeks of Liu's death, the FBI identified his killers as Ch'en Ch'i-li, Wu Tun, and Tung Kuei-sen, all three members of a gang called the United Bamboo (Chu Lien Pang), with branches both in the ROC and the United States. All three had fled from the United States to Taiwan after committing the crime. On November 17, 1984, acting on FBI information, police authorities on Taiwan arrested Ch'en and Wu. Tung, hearing he was wanted, had fled to the Philippines.

According to testimony by William Brown, senior deputy assistant secretary of state for Asian and Pacific affairs, it was not until sometime in December that the State Department was briefed by the FBI as to the facts in the case.[15] At that point, the State Department, acting through AIT, contacted "the highest level" of CCNAA to request cooperation. Cooperation was speedily given. Photographs and fingerprint records of those arrested were provided by ROC authorities, and agreement was given for Department of Justice officials to interview and polygraph them. This was done on January 22 and 23, 1985. By that time, there were even bigger fish in the net. The ROC authorities had arrested Admiral Wang Hsi-ling and his two deputies, Hu Yi-min and Ch'en Hu-men, for having instigated the assassination plot.

Requests were made that Ch'en and Wu (along with Tung, should he be apprehended) be sent to the United States for trial. In the absence of a pre-1979 extradition treaty between the United States and the ROC or a post-1979 agreement between AIT and CCNAA on extradition, this request was denied. Instead, Ch'en, Wu, Wang, Hu, and the second Ch'en were tried, convicted, and sentenced to prison terms on Taiwan, terms that they are still serving.[16] Ironically, it seems that the ROC had pressed on several occasions after 1979 for an extradition agreement between AIT and CCNAA. In making the request, the ROC indicated that it was interested primarily in extraditing persons accused of economic crimes. However, the United States had been unwilling to conclude such an agreement for fear that the ROC would attempt to use it to force the return of members of the Taiwan Independence Movement to the ROC.

What is striking about the Henry Liu affair is that both sides moved swiftly and surely to deal with the issue and to prevent it from damaging the U.S.-ROC relationship. For the ROC, there was ample reason for full cooperation. A 1981 amendment to the Arms Export Control Act prohibits arms sales to countries that engage in a consistent pattern of harrassment or intimidation of U.S. citizens. Clearly, it was in Taipei's interest to cooperate in the investigation of the Liu murder case in order to prove its good faith.

It seems equally clear, on the basis of testimony by then Deputy Assistant Secretary of State for East Asia and Pacific Affairs William Brown, that the U.S. executive branch did not wish to see relationships with the ROC damaged by the Henry Liu case and had no desire to reach a finding that would require terminating arms sales. Given these shared objectives, the absence of formal diplomatic relations proved no hindrance, which once again established that common interests are more important than formal diplomatic mechanisms. The ROC responded quickly and positively to U.S. requests, except the one asking for Ch'en and Wu to be extradited to the United States. Since the ROC had asked several times for an extradition agreement and the United States had balked, Taipei cannot really be faulted for this refusal.

Deputy Assistant Secretary Brown several times asserted in his testimony that all communications passed between AIT and CCNAA. Since this was a formal public hearing, he hardly could have said anything else. Private sources available to the author stated that, although it is true that all formal communications between the two governments were between AIT and CCNAA, conversations between Brown and Chien were frequent during this period. When there are important matters that need to be settled, the two sides understand there is no substitute for direct discussion.

The Taiwan Relations Act in Retrospect

Relations between the United States and the ROC have always had an emotional underpinning that made them unlike U.S. relations with most other countries. The World War II alliance, personal links between policy makers, and the presence of a large Chinese community in the United States with ties to the ROC made the period of formal diplomatic relationship unique. Only the U.S. relationship with Israel contains as much emotional resonance.

The TRA is the talisman of this unique relationship. It provides the functional equivalent of a defense treaty and does so by an act of Congress overriding the objections of the executive branch of government—which, under the Constitution and by precedent, had the authority to negotiate such treaties alone. Moreover, it extends this security commitment to a government and a state that is no longer recognized. It provides that, for all purposes of U.S. law, the authorities of the ROC shall continue to be considered a formally recognized, friendly government. Arms will (not *may:* the Act says *will*) continue to be sold to the ROC, and this necessarily has meant continuation of close connections between the U.S. and ROC military establishments. The instrumentalities created by the two sides operate as embassies and consulates in everything but name; they even negotiate agreements on behalf of their governments. The Act and the relationship it created are wholly without precedent in international relations.

The TRA formula succeeded because it had to; there was too much at stake for either side to let it fail. For the ROC, despite deep feelings of betrayal and pain, it was necessary to recement a relationship with its chief trading partner and the principal guarantor of its independence. For the United States, to the reality of a large and growing economic and commercial relationship was added Congress's feeling that the ROC had been ill used by the Carter administration and that a new relationship had to be made to protect the ROC and its people.

The relationship has worked. Trade figures tell some of the story: Between 1978 and 1988, two-way trade grew from $9 billion to $36.43 billion, and direct U.S. investment on Taiwan increased more than four times, from $500 million to $2.46 billion. Commercial relationships of this size and complexity bring numerous problems. Yet, the framework the Act created was broad enough, the AIT-CCNAA channel was flexible enough, and the mutuality of interests was sufficiently clear that problems could be addressed meaningfully and effectively. This does not mean that they could be solved in every case, but this is true as well of normal diplomatic relations, as witness the continuing trade problems with Japan.

Indeed, in some respects the AIT-CCNAA channel makes it easier to focus on the substance of problems and reach solutions. U.S. government departments tend to be rather sloppy about keeping written records of negotiations, whereas the Chinese keep meticulous records. In the past, U.S. officials negotiating with the ROC often were at a disadvantage as a result. However, because of its need to function as an agent of others, AIT has had to be equally meticulous about record keeping, and thus it is possible to trace accurately what has been said on any issue since AIT's inception. In addition, all too often U.S. delegations negotiating trade problems have been headed by political appointees who were barely acquainted with either the problem or its

past history and were interested more in quick fixes to achieve head-
lines back home than concrete and lasting results. By making sure that
officers familiar with the problem and its past history are part of the
negotiating team, the AIT mechanism ameliorates the problem of the
novice negotiator, although it does not eliminate the problem entirely.

But trade problems and their solutions are only part of the story.
The two sides did not become isolated from each other after the break
in formal diplomatic relations. Indeed, Dr. Frederick Chien, director
of CCNAA from 1983 to 1988, enjoyed far broader and more intensive access to senior policy makers in Washington than did James
Shen, the last ROC ambassador. And certainly David Dean's access to
ROC officials is every bit as good as was that of Leonard Unger, the
last U.S. ambassador in Taipei. After a hiatus of some years at the
beginning of the new relationship, State Department officials at the
office director level now visit Taiwan for conversations at the ROC
Foreign Ministry. Viewed in this light, the institutional framework
created under the TRA has been successful.

Of course, there have been areas of particular tension. As noted,
trade is one. Arms sales are another. Although Beijing has consistently
attacked the TRA as being completely inconsistent with the understandings that led to normalization of relations and as interference in
China's internal affairs, it has objected most strenuously to Section 3,
which provides that arms sales are to continue. In particular, Beijing
was determined to use every means at its disposal to block U.S. sale
of an advanced fighter to the ROC. Given the interest of Secretary of
State Alexander Haig in achieving what he referred to as a "strategic
relationship" with the PRC, Beijing's threats to freeze its relationship
with the United States and thaw its relationship with Moscow were
successful. In January 1982, the Reagan administration announced that
it would not sell an advanced fighter to the ROC.[17]

Having prevailed once, Beijing used the same threats to try to maneuver the United States into drastically reducing sales of other arms
to the ROC. This time it achieved a partial, yet still very significant
success. As noted earlier, in the joint communique of August 17, 1982,
the Reagan administration pledged itself to gradually reduce the
amount of arms sold the ROC, "leading over a period of time to a
final resolution." It also agreed to consult with Beijing on matters of
common interest, presumably including arms sales to the ROC.

In effect, the August 17 communique overrides Section 3's provision that the United States will continue to sell the ROC the weapons
required to defend itself against the PRC and will do so solely on the
basis of the ROC's needs. As Senator John Glenn said at the time,

"Not only do these restrictions contravene the spirit and purpose of the TRA, they are exactly the sort of PRC imposed conditions we sought to avoid when we drafted the Act."[18]

As matters have turned out, the August 17 communique, along with the ROC's ouster from the World Bank and the International Monetary Fund, proved to be Beijing's only success in the struggle to roll back the guarantees and special status given the ROC under the TRA. Although the PRC continues from time to time to demand the Act's amendment or replacement, by 1988 these calls had become so perfunctory that, in a visit to Washington in March of that year, former Foreign Minister Wu Hsueh-ch'uan did not even raise the issue.[19]

Interestingly enough, the PRC has never objected to specific operations of either AIT or CCNAA, despite the fact that they include governmental acts. It has been quick to protest matters of form, however, such as occasions on which state or municipal governments have allowed display of the ROC flag.

We can reasonably conclude that, in the conduct of trade—the ROC's economic lifeblood—the mechanism created by the TRA has worked very well. The same might be said of most other matters that involve the daily life of the people in both the ROC and the United States. All essential consular activities are performed easily and expeditiously. There has been no diminution in the number of ROC citizens traveling to the United States, and vice versa.

There is one area where the TRA has worked less well. As we have noted, in agreeing to the August 17, 1982 joint communique with Beijing, the Reagan administration in effect overrode the spirit if not precisely the letter of the TRA. Still, this cannot really be considered a fault of the TRA itself. The Constitution gives the executive branch plenipotentiary power in foreign affairs, and it is constitutionally or legally difficult for any piece of legislation to prevent an executive from carrying out some specific foreign policy. The history of the War Powers Act bears out this observation.

Even as amended by the August 17 communique, it seems that the TRA meets the interests of all three parties well enough that none wishes to upset the present balance by reopening the matter. In the United States, Democrats as well as Republicans, conservatives as well as liberals, members of Congress and executives of the administration take the attitude, "It's not broken, so let's not try to fix it." Both Taipei and Beijing seem to fear that opening the TRA to amendment could lead to results that would be more adverse to their interests.

Operating practice under the TRA could be changed, however. Since all sides have agreed to the polite fiction that CCNAA is a private body, there does not seem to be any logical reason why its director in Washington could not call on U.S. government officials in their offices. Doing so would allow problems to be addressed more quickly and possibly more effectively.

Fortunately for all, the TRA never became involved in the politics of the 1988 election year. Neither of the major candidates for the 1988 presidential election referred to the Act in a campaign statement, and there did not appear to be any reason why they or their party's platform should have done so. As the 1990s begin, the Act now is not only above politics, it is also seen as simply part of our contemporary reality. Students of law or international relations may marvel at its uniqueness or discuss the precedents it has created. Politicians, businessmen, and the public generally just accept it.

Notes

1. The author was director of the Office of Republic of China Affairs in the State Department from September 1977 until the office became the Taiwan Coordination Staff after January 1, 1979. He continued as coordinator for Taiwan until June 1979. Material on the Vance visit to Beijing in August 1977, and much of the information that follows, is drawn from the author's personal recollections and contemporaneous notes as well as from Secretary Vance's book *Hard Choices* (New York: Simon and Schuster, 1983). Teng Hsiao-p'ing's comments on the Vance visit as a retrograde step were published in the *Washington Post,* September 7, 1977. Secretary Vance's recollection of Teng's statements to him are given in *Hard Choices,* p. 83.

2. For Nixon's promises to the PRC on normalization, see Ralph N. Clough, *Island China* (Cambridge, Mass.: Harvard University Press, 1979), p. 204. For Ford, see Jaw-ling Joanne Chang, *United States–China Normalization: An Evaluation of Foreign Policy Decision Making* (Denver, Colo.: University of Denver, Graduate School of International Studies, Monograph Series in World Affairs, 1986), p. 164. The reaction of Carter administration officials is based on the author's recollections.

3. When the author began his service as director of the Office of Republic of China Affairs in September 1977, as a specific assignment he was ordered to design ways of accomplishing these purposes with respect to Taiwan in a manner that would allow normalization with the PRC to proceed, *i.e.,* to come up with a method for adapting the Japanese model in a way that would meet U.S. needs yet still not be so offensive to Beijing as to block normalization.

4. The Dole-Stone amendment to the International Security Assistance Act of 1978, signed into law by President Carter, provided that, since the Senate had given its advice and consent to the mutual defense treaty with the Republic of China in 1955, the president should not take action to terminate the treaty without first consulting the Congress. Nevertheless, even though the president had signed the International Security Assistance Act with the amendment, it was decided that the likelihood of leakage was too great, and therefore Congress was kept informed of progress toward PRC normalization only in a perfunctory way and was never really consulted. By adding to the TRA so many features objectionable to the Carter administration, the Congress was getting back its own.

5. For a thorough study of all the congressional debate and comment on the TRA, including pertinent portions of the House and Senate Reports as well as the text of the law itself, see Lester L. Wolff and David L. Simon, *Legislative History of the Taiwan Relations Act* (Jamaica, N.Y.: American Association for Chinese Studies, 1982).

6. Ibid., p. 13.

7. The debate outlined in this and the preceding paragraph is reconstructed from the author's recollections and notes.

8. The author was picketed by one such group when speaking at the University of Washington in Seattle in March 1979.

9. The description of the negotiations in the following paragraphs is based on the author's recollections and notes.

10. Data in this and the following paragraph come from an interview with AIT's senior consular officer, Thomas Hutson, conducted in Taipei, June 2, 1988.

11. These are the unanimous comments of four AIT officers interviewed in Taipei, June 1988.

12. Information in these paragraphs is based on interviews with Joseph B. Kyle, deputy director of AIT Washington on April 14, 1988; with David Dean, director of AIT Taipei on May 31, 1988; and with Philip Lincoln, economic officer of AIT Taipei on June 6, 1988.

13. Information on CCNAA Washington operations is drawn from an interview with its deputy director, Cheng Chien-jen (usually known as C. J. Chen), April 14, 1988, as well as from personal observations.

14. Material in this paragraph is derived mostly from an interview with Philip Lincoln, economic officer, AIT, Taipei, June 6, 1988.

15. Brown's testimony, together with a wealth of other material on the Henry Liu case, is to be found in U.S. Congress, House of Representatives, "The Murder of Henry Liu," *Hearings and Markup before the Committee on Foreign Affairs and the Subcommittee on Asian and Pacific Affairs, House of Representatives, 99th Congress, First Session, on H. Con. Res. 49 and 110, February 7, March 21, and April 3, 1985* (Washington, D.C., Government Printing Office, 1985), p. 36.

16. Wu Kuei-sen, having been extradited from Brazil, where he went after the Philippines, was tried and convicted of murder in California in June 1988.

17. For the text of the Reagan administration announcement, see the U.S. Department of State press release of January 11, 1982. The text emphasizes that there is no present military threat to Taiwan and that its air defense needs can continue to be met by further production of the venerable F-5 series interceptors, designed in the 1950s.

18. See Wolff and Simon, *Legislative History of the Taiwan Relations Act,* pp. 326–28.

19. Information provided to the author by State Department officials who participated in the talks.

ROBERT SUTTER

The Taiwan Relations Act and the United States' China Policy

WHEN THE TAIWAN RELATIONS ACT (TRA) became law in April 1979, debate raged in the U.S. Congress, and Congress and the Carter administration quarreled over U.S. policy toward the People's Republic of China (PRC) and Taiwan. U.S. policy makers in the administration and the Congress disagreed about the proper U.S. posture in this triangular relationship. As in the case of many such international triangles, the participants often tended to view it as a kind of zero-sum game.[1]

Thus, whenever the U.S. government attempted to interpret the TRA or take other actions designed to foster good relations with the PRC, such action often was seen by U.S. supporters of Taiwan as having an indirect but strong negative effect on U.S. interests vis-a-vis Taiwan. Similarly, whenever the U.S. government attempted to implement the TRA or take other steps designed to consolidate or improve relations with Taiwan, this often was seen by supporters of closer U.S.-PRC relations as having a strong negative effect on U.S. relations with the PRC.

The stakes in this U.S. policy debate are high. Supporters of Taiwan have often demonstrated considerable anxiety that U.S. cutbacks in relations with Taiwan would reach a point where Taiwan's security, stability, and economic prosperity are endangered. Other U.S. officials have stressed the need to implement the TRA so as to cut back U.S.-

Taiwan relationships in order to improve U.S.-PRC relations. In particular, they warned that to do otherwise would call into question the U.S. position in a larger and strategically more important triangular relationship, namely, the U.S.-Soviet-Chinese great power triangle. Not surprisingly, they have tended to view relations within this great power triangle as a zero-sum game. They have argued that U.S.-PRC friction over Taiwan and other issues blocked the ability of the United States to move ahead with relations with the PRC and thereby gain a perceived advantage for the United States against the Soviet Union.

In 1979, there was much anxiety in the United States that the PRC might become alienated from the United States and seek to improve ties with the Soviet Union. Many perceived the United States as being in a comparatively weak strategic position vis-a-vis the Soviet Union. In the late 1970s, the Soviet Union was repeatedly expanding its influence in the Third World through military and other means. The United States was having considerable difficulty in meeting the Soviet challenge, and U.S. allies were less than effective in supplementing U.S. efforts to meet the challenge. Given these developments, many argued that the United States should have closer relations with the PRC to compensate for the United States' decline relative to the Soviet Union.

However, U.S. policy concerns regarding implementation of the TRA and, more broadly, concerns over U.S. policy regarding the PRC and Taiwan were influenced by a wide range of factors, not just the U.S. triangular relations with Beijing and Taipei and with Beijing and Moscow. Indeed, we shall see later how executive-congressional consultation over policy changes had a great deal to do with the policy debate over the TRA in the late 1970s and early 1980s. Yet it remains a fact that the policy debate over implementation of the TRA was influenced by the differing perceptions of appropriate U.S. interests in these two triangular relationships.

The division between the Carter administration and the Congress on the appropriate U.S. position in these two triangular relationships was not clear-cut. However, Congress generally opposed Carter administration efforts that were seen to cut back U.S. ties with Taiwan and improve relations with the PRC for the sake of a perceived advantage in U.S. relations in the Sino-Soviet-U.S. triangle.

During the early years of the Reagan administration, the policy debate shifted to groups focused within the administration, where strong advocates of a position favoring the PRC in both triangular relationships encountered strong opposition, especially from supporters of President Reagan who felt that the United States should sustain close ties with and strong backing for Taiwan. Members of Congress with close ties to the president and his conservative constituency also played an important role in mid 1982 in tipping the policy debate away from positions favoring the PRC at Taiwan's expense.

Since about 1983, U.S. policy makers have shown much less contention and urgency over implementation of the TRA because of less worry over these issues in the two triangular relationships. Of course, policy makers remain sensitive to these relationships, and some still view them as largely zero-sum games. But the consequences of possible shifts in these triangular relationships generally are seen to have much less urgent or profound consequences for U.S. interests than in the recent past. Indeed, certain aspects of these triangular relationships have begun to look more like a positive sum game than a zero sum game. This new view has paved the way for a general consensus on U.S. policy toward China and Taiwan and implementation of the TRA. Even strong supporters of Taiwan in the U.S. Congress are less concerned that the United States will try to improve relations with the PRC at the expense of Taiwan's security, stability, or economic prosperity. They also concede that the TRA deals effectively with new problems in U.S.-Taiwan relations—the large U.S. trade deficit with Taiwan, possible political instability following the death of President Chiang Ching-kuo, and prospects for political liberalization and democracy on the island.

Even on more sensitive political and military issues in U.S.-PRC-Taiwan relations, many believe that U.S. policy has achieved an appropriate balance. The United States has offered to sell advanced fighter aircraft equipment to the PRC without causing a major stir among Taiwan supporters in the United States. At the same time, the United States allows U.S. companies to provide technology, advice, and support to Taiwan's development of an advanced fighter aircraft without prompting much reaction from those who fear that such a step alienates the PRC and jeopardizes developing closer U.S.-PRC ties to counter Soviet international expansion.

Developments that have prompted a less urgent and contentious climate for U.S. policy toward China and Taiwan have included:

1. Increased U.S. confidence in dealing with the Soviet Union and recognizing that China has less strategic importance for the United States. U.S. policy makers have acquired more confidence in recent years in their ability to deal with the geopolitical challenges posed by the Soviet Union without having to encourage the more active cooperation of China. The United

States has improved its military and political capability to match
the Soviet Union's projection of power because of the large-scale
buildup of the U.S. military during the Reagan administration
and the internal and international difficulties now faced by the
Soviet Union. U.S. allies became more united in their willingness to work more closely with the United States to counter the
Soviet Union, especially in Asia, where Japanese Prime Minister
Nakasone took initiatives to strengthen Japan's defenses.

Japan and other U.S. allies and friends along the periphery of
Asia have become more important to the United States in protecting the Western Pacific and Indian Ocean communications
routes from a new Soviet military challenge. China has become
less important in dealing with the perceived Soviet danger.

Meanwhile, the PRC's leadership expressed satisfaction with
the existing balance in Asian and world affairs and is less interested in having closer strategic ties with the United States
against the Soviet Union. Instead, the PRC has favored an independent posture in foreign affairs, preferring to ease tensions
with the Soviet Union while maintaining close ties with the
United States, Japan, and other important noncommunist countries. Consequently, U.S. policy makers no longer believed it
necessary to press for a cutback in U.S. ties with Taiwan to keep
Beijing on the U.S. side to oppose the USSR.

2. Increased U.S. confidence in Asian stability. During the
1970s, many worried that Asian peace and stability were in jeopardy. The U.S.-backed governments in Cambodia and South
Vietnam had collapsed; U.S. forces might be withdrawn from
South Korea; bitter controversy surrounded the U.S. decision to
normalize diplomatic relations with Beijing and break official ties
with Taiwan; and the United States responded weakly to the
Soviet-backed Vietnamese invasion of Cambodia and the Soviet
invasion of Afghanistan.

By the late 1980s, however, U.S. observers saw Asia as stable
and at peace. The United States had more confidence in its ability to check Soviet expansion. The PRC leaders remained committed to political and economic reforms to promote economic
modernization and national development. Chinese relations with
Japan and other noncommunist Asian states had improved, and
Beijing seemed less inclined to revert to past practice of disrupting Asian stability and threatening its noncommunist neighbors.
Beijing had even moderated its policy toward Taiwan. After demanding more U.S. concessions concerning Taiwan following

the release of the August 1982 U.S.-PRC communique on U.S. arms sales to Taiwan, Beijing decided to move forward in other areas of U.S.-PRC relations while guarding against any U.S. backsliding on existing commitments regarding Taiwan.

Taiwan, for its part, had weathered the political difficulties of the 1970s and had become a new power in international trade. It was now one of the top five U.S. trading partners and held one of the world's largest foreign exchange reserves. Its authoritarian government had eased political control and allowed more interchange with the mainland.

These trends reduced the zero-sum quality of the U.S.-PRC-Taiwan triangular relationship. In fact, the Beijing-Taipei leg of the triangle became less tense as trade, travel, and other communications developed across the Taiwan Strait. In this context, the United States had greater leeway to develop relations with Taiwan under the auspices of the TRA without prompting a negative reaction from the PRC.

3. Maturity in the formulation of U.S. China policy. One result of the tense U.S. interactions with PRC and Taiwan officials during the late 1970s and early 1980s was that U.S. policy makers were repeatedly exposed to strong demands from both Beijing and Taipei. Gradually, those who had tended to strongly favor either the PRC or Taiwan side of the U.S.-PRC-Taiwan triangle moderated their positions and sought a middle course.

Taiwan demanded that the Reagan administration provide U.S. F-16 aircraft. That fighter was among the most advanced in the U.S. Air Force inventory. Selling that fighter would not only have enraged the PRC but also upset the prevailing military balance in the Taiwan Strait. Many U.S. policy makers believed Taiwan's demand for the F-16 to be excessive; in fact, that demand even alienated some U.S. policy makers who were pushing to upgrade the quality of the U.S. fighters provided to Taiwan. In the end, Taiwan was granted access only to the same fighter (the F-5E) it had previously received.

The PRC, meanwhile, demanded that the United States limit U.S. arms sales to Taiwan, based on their interpretation of the August 17, 1982, U.S.-PRC joint communique. The PRC also complained about U.S. economic, trade, and other policies. In response, U.S. policy makers recoiled from these demands; they called Beijing's bluff to threaten to downgrade the U.S.-PRC relationship. The PRC then backed away from its threats and sought to consolidate relations with the United States.

4. Increased continuity and a better understanding of U.S. China policy. U.S. China policy has stabilized in recent years, as compared with the late 1970s and early 1980s. The China policy of the late 1970s and early 1980s proved to be too abrupt, was conducted in secrecy, and was marred by acrimony between Congress and the executive branch over how these two branches should formulate China policy. By contrast, U.S. policy makers in the Reagan administration have been able to consult with relevant U.S. interest groups, including those represented in the Congress, to build better understanding of that policy. These developments made it easier to build a policy consensus on China and Taiwan and to implement the TRA.

Controversy Over the Taiwan Relations Act During the Carter Administration

Concerns regarding implementation of the TRA were expressed most strongly in the period immediately following passage of the Act. The Carter administration's decision to switch official ties from Taipei to Beijing and the broader implications of the administration's tilt toward the PRC engendered intense debate concerning the two triangular relationships.

President Carter's surprise announcement on December 15, 1978, that the United States would establish diplomatic relations with the People's Republic of China as of January 1, 1979, would break its diplomatic ties with the Nationalist Chinese administration on Taiwan on that day, and would terminate its defense treaty with Taiwan a year later presented the United States, especially the U.S. Congress, with new legal, economic, and strategic problems regarding future U.S. relations with the PRC and Taiwan. President Carter wanted to remove the Taiwan issue as an impediment to normal U.S.-PRC diplomatic relations. The issue of Taiwan had remained the major stumbling block between Washington and Beijing following President Nixon's landmark visit to the PRC in February 1972. During the next five years, the Nixon and Ford administrations had emphasized common U.S.-PRC strategic interests in opposition to Soviet superpower "hegemony" and had encouraged closer contacts with the PRC without substantially changing formal U.S. diplomatic and defense ties and the rapidly growing economic and cultural relations with Taiwan.

Beijing's leaders continually demanded during this period that the United States meet three conditions for the normalization of U.S.-PRC diplomatic relations: The United States must withdraw all military forces from Taiwan, break diplomatic relations with the government on Taiwan, and terminate the U.S.-Taiwan defense treaty. At the same time, Beijing's leaders urged the United States to follow the example of Japan's normalization of relations with the PRC in September 1972. Adopting the "Japanese formula" would require that the United States end diplomatic relations with the Taipei government, recognize Beijing as the sole legal government of China, and acknowledge Beijing's claim that Taiwan was part of China. This formula would also terminate the U.S.-Taiwan defense treaty, but U.S. economic relations with Taiwan could continue unhindered, and political relations with Taiwan would be maintained through private offices staffed by career foreign service officers who were officially retired, separated, or on leave.

President Carter's normalization announcement presented Congress with the following questions:

1. How would the United States continue arms sales and commercial, cultural, and other forms of interchange with Taiwan after breaking off official relations?

2. What legislative actions would be required to normalize commercial and other interchanges with the PRC following the normalization of diplomatic relations?

3. What should be the direction of future U.S. policy toward the PRC, and what effect would changed relations with Beijing have on important U.S. foreign and defense concerns?

President Carter made clear that the United States would meet Beijing's three conditions and that it would follow, with few modifications, the Japanese formula on normalization. The United States did not immediately terminate the U.S.-Taiwan defense treaty. Instead, Washington gave Taiwan a one-year notice that the mutual defense treaty would be terminated, in accord with the treaty's provisions. In addition, the United States announced that it expected the Taiwan issue to be settled peacefully. Administration officials told the press after the president's announcement that the United States would continue to deliver military equipment already contracted for to Taiwan during 1979 and that, even after formal military ties ended, the United States would continue to make available to Taiwan "selected defense weap-onry" on a "restricted basis."[2]

The Carter administration subsequently prepared a package of legislation to govern future relations with Taiwan and submitted it to Congress in January 1979.[3] As with the Japanese formula, this pro-posal called for the establishment of a nonprofit private corporation, to be called the American Institute in Taiwan (AIT), that would carry out programs, transactions, and other relations previously conducted by the U.S. embassy. The Institute would receive government funds to carry out its functions and would be staffed by personnel separated from government service but eligible for reinstatement with full ca-reer benefits after their employment with AIT ended.

The proposed Taiwan Omnibus Bill also provided that the people on Taiwan would not be denied eligibility for U.S. programs that le-gally required the maintenance of diplomatic relations with the United States and specified that laws, regulations, and orders related to foreign governments would continue to apply to Taiwan. These provisions confirmed Taiwan's continued eligibility under the Arms Export Control Act, the Export-Import Bank Act, the Foreign Assis-tance Act of 1961, and other legislation.

Congressional reaction to the administration's proposed legislation was mixed. Most members of Congress believed that special congres-sional efforts were needed to modify the administration's new policy toward the PRC and Taiwan. Few members opposed the establish-ment of diplomatic relations with Beijing because most agreed with the administration's argument that this was a goal that had been widely accepted in the United States since President Nixon's trip to the PRC in 1972. They were more concerned over the administration's inadequate handling of the timing and method of normalization and especially its effect on Taiwan and other U.S. foreign policy issues. Here, the members of Congress contended that the administration had not done a good job.[4]

During the debate on the Taiwan bill, Congress registered its dis-satisfaction and proposed numerous amendments. Besides focusing on future U.S. relations with Taiwan, Congress also showed concern over U.S. policy toward the PRC and Asia and over the problems and prospects of congressional-executive interaction in the conduct of U.S. foreign policy.

Many members of Congress were especially critical of the Carter administration's haste and secrecy in coming to an agreement with the PRC. The administration's lack of consultation was resented because only a few months earlier Congress had passed an amendment to the

International Security Assistance Act of 1978 (Public law 95–384) expressing its sense that the president should consult with Congress before he made any policy changes that might affect the mutual defense treaty with Taiwan.[5]

Some members became even more irritated with the administration when its representatives, at hearings on the Taiwan bill, implied that Congress should complete work on the bill before March 1, 1979, because at that time official ties between the United States and Taiwan would be completely cut off after a two-month adjustment period, and without the new legislation those ties would have no secure basis for continuing.[6] This news was especially unsatisfactory inasmuch as the administration did not submit its proposed bill to Congress until late in January. House Foreign Affairs Committee Chairman Clement Zablocki remarked to his colleagues that they were working "under the gun" of this administration-imposed deadline.[7] Meanwhile, several congressional officials were furious when President Carter repeatedly warned them that he would veto the Taiwan legislation—and thereby risk disrupting relations with Taipei—if Congress altered the administration-proposed bill in a way that the president judged to be inconsistent with the agreement he had reached with the PRC.[8]

Against this background of congressional-executive friction, Congress set to work to modify several substantive aspects of the Taiwan bill. In broad terms, Congress thought that the bill gave too little attention to U.S. security interests in Taiwan and the Western Pacific, failed to treat adequately future U.S.-Taiwan economic relations, slighted several important legal questions regarding relations with Taiwan, and avoided providing for strong congressional oversight of U.S.-Taiwan ties.[9] Let us consider some of these issues of disagreement in more detail.

Security Issues

Congress was particularly concerned that the official U.S. break with Taiwan might be misinterpreted in Asia and elsewhere as a breach of U.S. commitments in East Asia after the U.S. had failed to defend South Vietnam. Some of its members judged that the Carter administration's failure to consult closely with U.S. allies in Asia before it announced the normalization decision could give the impression that the United States was not concerned with the fate of its friends and would not provide future security support.[10] After heated discussion over several different proposals in both houses, Congress decided to amend the Taiwan bill to demonstrate more clearly the U.S.

commitment to support the security of people on Taiwan and to maintain an active interest in backing U.S. allies elsewhere in the region. In Sections 2 and 3 of the bill, Congress added several policy declarations affirming, among other things, that it was the policy of the United States:

- To declare that the peace and security of the Western Pacific are in the interests of the United States;
- To make clear that the United States expects that the future of Taiwan will be determined by peaceful means;
- To consider any nonpeaceful effort against Taiwan—including boycotts and embargoes—as a threat to the peace of the Western Pacific and of grave concern to the United States;
- To provide Taiwan with enough defensive arms to maintain a sufficient self-defense capability; and
- To maintain the capacity of the United States to resist any resort to force or other coercion that would jeopardize Taiwan's well-being.

To ensure that this policy was fully carried out, Congress specified that it, along with the president, would determine the types and quantities of defensive arms and services to be provided to Taiwan and required that the president promptly inform the Congress of any threat to Taiwan's security.

Economic and Legal Questions

In view of the speed and secrecy surrounding the administration's final decision on normalization, many in Congress believed that most executive branch officials with knowledge of Chinese affairs were unprepared to deal with the complicated economic and legal questions involved in future U.S. relations with the PRC and Taiwan. During hearings on the Taiwan bill, several members of Congress voiced concern that the administration had not consulted with U.S. economic leaders and legal experts with extensive experience in dealing with the PRC and Taiwan to establish a mechanism for maintaining stable economic and legal ties with Taiwan after establishing diplomatic ties with the PRC. Congress solicited the opinions of many such leaders and experts and then adopted numerous changes in the legislation to enable the United States to have legal relations but no formal diplomatic ties with Taiwan.

To help safeguard U.S.-Taiwan economic relations, Congress added provisions that allowed U.S. investors in Taiwan to continue to receive guarantees from the Overseas Private Investment Council (OPIC), even though Taiwan's annual per capita income of about $1,300 surpassed the $1,000 ceiling normally imposed by OPIC at that time. Congress also inserted language that specifically continued the transfer of nuclear power supplies and technology to Taiwan, added the previously noted wording specifying U.S. opposition to embargoes and boycotts of Taiwan, and specified that the end of official U.S. ties with Taiwan should not be seen as a basis for supporting the exclusion of that state from continued membership in international financial institutions or other international organizations.

To protect U.S. legal ties with Taiwan, Congress adopted provisions explicitly affirming that state's ability to sue and be sued in U.S. courts, specified how Taiwan should be treated under terms of the Immigration and Nationality Act, and set forth in more detail the services to be provided by the AIT to U.S. citizens living in Taiwan. Congress also asked the president to grant Taiwan's counterpart to the AIT—the Coordinating Council for North American Affairs (CCNAA)—the same number of offices in the United States as the Taipei government had held before January 1, 1979, and authorized the president to grant privileges and immunities to CCNAA personnel in the United States equivalent to those granted AIT personnel in Taiwan. Congress held that the U.S. switch in recognition should not be seen as affecting Taiwan's assets in the United States, a provision that governed the sensitive issue of Chinese diplomatic property in the United States. Congress also added a precise definition of the term *Taiwan* to include the governing authorities on the island recognized by the United States prior to January 1, 1979.

Finally, because human rights in Taiwan were repeatedly mentioned during the course of the hearings and deliberations on the bill, Congress added a provision to Section 2 of the Act reaffirming U.S. interest in human rights on Taiwan and asserting that nothing in the Act opposed that interest.

Congressional Oversight

Worried by the administration's failure to consult fully with Congress and by the omission of specific references to Congress's role in future U.S.-Taiwan relations when the administration proposed its legislation, Congress added several amendments that explicitly granted Congress a strong role in the oversight and supervision of future U.S. relations with Taiwan. Not only did Congress add language requiring the president to promptly inform it of any threat to Taiwan, but it also set up other reporting procedures. Section 12 of the Act stated that agreements made by the AIT would be subject to congressional notification, review, and approval procedures and that the secretary of state would be required to make semiannual reports to Congress on the status of U.S.-Taiwan relations for two years after the Act became effective. In addition, the president should report to Congress any rules and regulations he might formulate for carrying out provisions of the TRA during a three-year period following the start of the Act. Section 14 noted that the House Foreign Affairs Committee, Senate Foreign Relations Committee, and other appropriate committees should monitor the implementation of the Act, the affairs of AIT, U.S.-Taiwan economic relations, and U.S. security policies in the Western Pacific.

Implementation of the Taiwan Relations Act

After passage of the TRA, many members of Congress criticized the Carter administration's handling of commercial and other agreements with Taiwan as well as its policy regarding arms sales to Taiwan. While debating the Taiwan bill, many in Congress contended that the administration was moving too far and too fast to favor the PRC. Congress was especially on guard against any administration efforts to cut back U.S. ties with Taiwan in order to improve U.S. relations with the PRC, which was seen by the administration leaders as a vital element in U.S. strategy to deal with the USSR.

Vice-President Walter Mondale disclosed in Canton, China, in August 1979 that the administration planned to end some commercial agreements with Taiwan and replace them with unofficial arrangements. To many observers in Taiwan and the United States, including several members of Congress, the vice-president's disclosure was a reversal of the administration's repeated assurances (given at the time of U.S.-PRC normalization) that all treaties and agreements between the United States and Taiwan, with the exception of the defense treaty, would remain in effect after formal ties had been established with the PRC. Administration officers countered that Congress was told during deliberations on the Taiwan bill that existing agreements with Taiwan would have to be altered eventually as they expired or became obsolete or irrelevant to U.S.-Taiwan relations. In response to congressional criticism on this issue, the administration clarified its position in late 1979, affirming that it did "not have a policy to convert or

terminate all the treaties and agreements we maintain with Taiwan,"
would adjust each agreement "as the circumstances require . . . on a
case-by-case basis," and would "maintain close contact with Congress
on this subject."[11]

In reviewing this episode during private interviews in 1980,[12] congressional staff and administration officials indicated that the quick and
forceful congressional response to Vice-President Mondale's announcement caught administration officials unprepared and made them defensive. They had to answer repeated congressional complaints that
the Carter administration had deliberately misled Congress earlier in
the year about the agreements with Taiwan in order to guarantee passage of the administration's Taiwan bill. Some administration officers
claimed that they had made clear to Congress during deliberations on
that legislation that some agreements with Taiwan would have to be
changed, and they pointed to language in the Act that implicitly gave
the administration the legal right to change the status of these accords.
Other administration officials acknowledged, however, that testimony
before Congress and other statements by administration leaders earlier
in 1979 clearly had given an impression that the status of these agreements would not be changed.

Congressional pressure ultimately forced the administration to
give ground. Carter administration representatives had to reassure
congressional leaders in several public pronouncements that the executive branch had no intention of converting or terminating all treaties
and agreements with Taiwan and that the administration would
consult closely with Congress if a particular agreement was converted
or ended. Administration officers judged that such statements served
to slow further efforts to change the status of U.S. agreements with
Taiwan.

Arms Sales to Taiwan

The Defense Department notified Congress in July 1979 that a
package of military equipment, mostly aircraft and missiles worth
about $240 million, was being forwarded to Taiwan, although the
normalization agreement with Beijing required that no new arms
deals should move ahead. In January 1980, the Defense Department
informed Congress of a package of new weapons worth about $280
million that it would be selling to Taiwan during the year.

Even though this package contained some sophisticated weapons,
various members of Congress criticized the administration because
these weapons did not guarantee Taiwan's defenses and the adminis-

tration had ignored Congress's desire to determine what U.S. arms would be sold to Taiwan. Congressional critics believed that the Act had granted Congress's wish to be consulted on weapons transfers before the executive branch notified the Defense Department. Administration representatives countered that they had complied with all legal requirements covering the arms transfers to Taiwan and that the TRA did not require any consultations with Congress on this matter. This dispute persisted into June 1980, when seven members of the Senate Foreign Relations Committee sent a letter to President Carter asking that U.S. companies be permitted to begin discussing the sale of advanced fighter aircraft (the FX) to Taiwan. The administration agreed to this proposal later that month.

In reviewing these episodes in subsequent private interviews, some congressional staff members thought that the administration should have consulted more closely with Congress about the sales because Congress had always been interested in maintaining the security of Taiwan and in selecting which U.S. arms should be transferred to the island. They charged that the administration ignored congressional concerns and provided no consultations on this issue, instead notifying Congress of the arms to be transferred and referring to laws other than the TRA. The timing of the administration's notification—shortly before the public announcement on January 4, 1980—also raised congressional questions about executive branch sincerity. There had been two previous major administration initiatives on the PRC and Taiwan issues, the December 1978 announcement of normalization and Vice-President Mondale's disclosure in August 1979 on ending official agreements with Taiwan. All three executive branch announcements had been made while Congress was out of session. Many members speculated that such timing was part of an administration effort to outmaneuver Congress's efforts to oppose the administration's conduct of foreign affairs.

Some administration officers said in private interviews that such congressional complaints were unjustified, charging that members and staffers in Congress were making excessive demands on the executive branch to consult about China policy. To these executive branch officials, Congress wanted the administration to forfeit its legal right to determine foreign affairs simply to have good relations with Congress. They insisted that the administration had followed all legal requirements in regard to arms transfers to Taiwan and that the TRA did not require the extraordinary consultations with Congress called for by these dissatisfied congressional officials.

Sources of Friction Over
the Taiwan Relations Act

The Secrecy Issue

When congressional and administration aides were asked to explain why the Carter administration had failed to cooperate with Congress in formulating China policy, an overwhelming majority mentioned the tight secrecy with which China policy had been conducted. They noted, for instance, that since the results of the U.S.-PRC negotiations on normalization were known to only a few administration officials before December 15, 1978, the administration was not prepared to deal adequately with Congress's subsequent requests for clarification. Although some legal preparation for the administration's Taiwan bill had been carried out in 1978, State Department legal experts could never draft the bill until full details of the U.S.-PRC negotiations had been given to them. Moreover, the extreme secrecy within the executive branch also caused administration officers to give members of Congress the erroneous impression that new arms sales to Taiwan would not be terminated during 1979 and that the United States would maintain all official agreements with Taiwan except the defense treaty.

Administration officers noted several reasons for the secrecy in China policy. Some stressed that the PRC leaders had demanded dealing with the United States in private rather than informing the world and the Chinese people how willing they were to compromise and collaborate with what Beijing had once referred to as "American imperialism." Others noted that U.S. China policy had always been highly secretive since the Nixon administration's opening to the PRC, and this practice was continued as Carter administration officials negotiated with the PRC.

According to some State Department officers, there were efforts early in the Carter administration to open China policy by presenting background briefings to the press on U.S.-PRC relations, but those briefings reportedly were later judged as having an adverse effect on U.S. interests, especially when a senior administration officer announced that Secretary Vance's August 1979 visit to China had achieved significant progress in the normalization of diplomatic relations, only to have Vice-Premier Teng Hsiao-p'ing publicly say that the Vance visit was a "step backward." According to these State Department aides, Teng rebuked the United States for leaking reports of the Vance negotiations. Teng's admission caused the administration, in the words of one official, to "circle the wagons" on China policy to avoid any further leaks.

Several officers in the State Department noted that the injunction against leaks was resented because the State Department had served as the administration's primary means of informing Congress and the press about foreign policy. However, policy planners in the White House had long assumed the State Department to be the source of unauthorized disclosures of information on sensitive issues. A few State Department officials resented White House pressure to conduct China policy in secret. They complained that it ran counter to keeping Congress adequately informed about developments in China policy. One official characterized White House aides as "obtuse" in their understanding of why the administration should consult with Congress on China policy.

Some administration and congressional sources claimed that White House pressures for secrecy led to unnecessary and unjustified friction between State Department officers working on China policy and their congressional counterparts. Yet these aides had no alternative because they were ordered by the White House to say nothing. Congress perceived State Department aides as arrogant and dishonest because they were unable to be frank about China policy in talks with Congress.

Among other reasons given for the covert approach in Chinese affairs was the need not to alarm the public lest normalization be derailed by a public outcry demanding no change in China policy. Secrecy was necessary to avoid a head-on confrontation with the emotionalism that had surrounded the China issue in U.S. politics. Moreover, the China lobby could block any attempt to cut ties with Taiwan, and a large proportion of the public did not support any break in official U.S.-Taiwan ties.

Congressional Weaknesses

Although the administration's handling of China policy received heavy criticism from many administration officers and from some congressional aides, these critics also pointed to certain failings on Congress's part, such as the lack of congressional responsibility for a China policy. Administration officials complained that, when they did consult with Congress after the normalization decision in late 1978, they often did not know which members and staff to consult. Both leaders of the full House and Senate needed to be contacted, as well as the leaders of the various congressional committees and subcommittees with oversight responsibilities for China. Meanwhile, members of Congress and the staff of committees who had formerly expressed an interest in China policy also had to be informed. Because the China issue was expected to greatly influence U.S. domestic politics, many other members of Congress wanted prompt and full information about the new policy. To inform all these groups was a task far beyond the capability of the few officers available in the State Department and elsewhere in the administration for such liaison work.

Some in the administration also charged that members of Congress and their staffs could not be expected to use sensitive foreign policy information in a sober and careful way that would not endanger U.S. interests. These critics suspected that many legislators and their staffs would use such information for narrow political interests, such as engaging in "demagoguery," "political grandstanding," or newspaper "headline hunting" for personal gain or for their constituents. Thus, administration officials insisted that they had to take prudent steps to make certain that China policy did not promote "partisanship" and "factional interests" in Congress. From the perspective of these administration officers, they would confide about Chinese affairs only in those few members of Congress and staffs they could "trust."

A final complaint voiced by some senior administration leaders was that Congress's constant demands to consult and be informed about China policy reflected part of a broader congressional effort in recent years to chip away at the authority of the president and restrict the executive branch's control over foreign affairs. They asserted that Congress was often "unreasonable" to demand clarification of China policy. Administration officials allegedly had the responsibility to resist or circumvent such congressional pressures, not only to help protect the administration's China policy but also to help preserve the constitutional rights of the executive branch and to safeguard the system of checks and balances in the government.

Controversy During the Reagan Administration

The passage of the TRA did not end controversy regarding U.S. relations with Taiwan. Indeed, U.S. policy toward Taiwan had been clouded by the passage of the Act. In establishing diplomatic relations with the PRC, the United States had agreed to recognize the PRC, to break official ties with Taiwan, and to terminate the defense treaty. The Carter administration also strongly reaffirmed U.S. adherence to the principle of "one China." Thus, it acknowledged the Chinese position that the Republic of China did not exist separately and was part of China, and it recognized the PRC as the sole legal government of China. To the Chinese and many international observers, the normalization communique meant that the United States expected Taiwan to be reunited eventually with the mainland. However, amended passages of the TRA altered such an interpretation of the normalization communique by clearly implying that the United States expected the Republic of China to exist and Taiwan to remain separate from the mainland under U.S. protection for the foreseeable future.

Beijing protested these amended passages even before the Act was passed. But U.S. citizens remained largely unaware of their importance until the Presidential campaign of 1980, when Ronald Reagan complained that the Carter administration had treated Taiwan shabbily. Reagan charged that the Carter administration had violated the TRA by placing restrictions on U.S. official discussions with representatives from Taiwan about U.S. arms transfers to the island and about the activities of Taiwan's representatives in the United States. Despite repeated complaints from Beijing, candidate Reagan went on to formulate a comprehensive statement on policy toward Taiwan that sidestepped what past U.S. statements really meant regarding the principle of one China. Reagan based his policy firmly on implementing the TRA.[13] As the new controversy heated up during the summer and fall of 1980, PRC and Carter administration spokespersons warned of the dire consequences for U.S.-PRC relations if Reagan became president and then upgraded U.S.-Taiwan relations according to his announced policy.

Downgrading U.S.-Taiwan Relations, 1981–1982

After taking office, President Reagan adopted a more ambiguous policy toward Taiwan. Although he continued to express support for the TRA, his administration stopped short of restoring official contacts with that government and set aside, at least for a time, Taiwan's request to upgrade the relationship and provide its defense system with sophisticated U.S. fighter aircraft and naval missiles. More important, Reagan administration spokespersons began to reaffirm the

U.S. commitments embodied in the U.S.-PRC normalization communique and repeatedly pledged to strive to improve relations with the PRC.

This approach did little to solve the continuing debate over U.S. policy toward Taiwan and how to implement the TRA. Most notably, the TRA still called for the United States to continue selling arms to Taiwan, and many supporters of Taiwan in the United States favored the sale of sophisticated weapons to the island. Beijing warned that China's tolerance of such sales was limited. In early 1981, Beijing downgraded diplomatic relations with the Netherlands after the Dutch government agreed to sell two submarines to Taiwan, and the PRC warned that similar actions would be taken against other countries that sold weapons to Taiwan. Later that year, Beijing toughened its policy and warned that any U.S. weapons sale to Taiwan would be a satisfactory reason to downgrade U.S.-PRC relations, unless the United States first agreed to stop all weapons sales to Taiwan over a period of several years.

The Reagan administration attempted to meet the new PRC demands while avoiding any weakening in U.S. ties with Taiwan or endangering the island's future. On January 11, 1982, the United States announced that there would be no sale of fighter aircraft more advanced that those already being provided to Taiwan. After several months of intensive negotiations, on August 17, 1982, the United States and the PRC issued a joint communique that established at least a temporary compromise over the arms sale question. As a result, two days later the administration announced, without prompting any hostile PRC response, the proposed sale of 60 F-5E/F aircraft to be co-produced in Taiwan from 1983 to 1986. Reaction to the communique was mixed, particularly among President Reagan's constituency in the Republican Party.

The PRC remained very sensitive over the Taiwan issue, demanding strict U.S. adherence to the communique and criticizing U.S. interpretations of that accord. An August 17 *People's Daily* editorial commenting on the accord warned that U.S.-PRC relations would "face another crisis" like the recent impasse over arms sales if U.S. leaders continued to adhere to the TRA, which Beijing called "the fundamental obstacle to the development of Sino-U.S. relations."

As a result of these events, U.S. supporters of Taiwan became particularly concerned over what they viewed as a new trend in U.S. policy toward the PRC and Taiwan. They interpreted U.S. policy as moving in the direction of meeting PRC demands and conditions while gradually cutting back contacts and ties with Taiwan simply for the sake of improved relations with the PRC. The new China policy seemed to place a strong emphasis on maintaining and building good relations with Beijing, for the sake of U.S. strategic interests regarding Asia and the USSR. Recent U.S. presidents—Republican and Democrat—appeared only too willing to implement the TRA in ways that would slowly cut back U.S. interactions with Taiwan to satisfy PRC demands.

Anxiety among U.S. supporters of Taiwan was not just focused on the issue of PRC pressure for a cutback in U.S. arms sales to Taiwan. Had the United States suddenly endangered Taiwan simply to satisfy PRC demands? Did both a letter by President Reagan to PRC leaders, released in May 1982, and the August 17, 1982 communique positively refer to recent PRC peace proposals to Taiwan? Would the United States eventually support Taiwan's reunification with the PRC on Beijing's terms? Finally, would the United States prevent Taiwan from taking steps to maintain its independence from the PRC? These questions voiced the fear that Beijing had forced the United States to force Taiwan to enter into peace negotiations on Beijing's terms. Meanwhile, U.S. pressure on Taiwan over bilateral trade disputes, human rights conditions, and the new leadership succession problem in Taipei took on a new sense of urgency for Taiwan supporters.[14]

The debate over Reagan administration policy toward the PRC and Taiwan and U.S. implementation of the TRA really raged within the administration rather than between the administration and Congress, as during the Carter years. After Reagan was elected, congressional supporters of Taiwan judged that the president was unlikely to implement or interpret the TRA in ways that would substantially undermine Taiwan's security and prosperity. Faced with strong PRC pressure and senior aides arguing for closer U.S. strategic relations with the PRC, President Reagan grudgingly gave ground by adopting policies that were more compatible with PRC demands and incompatible with the aims of his supporters who strongly defended the TRA. The matter came to a head in early 1982 over the FX decision and, later in mid 1982, over the August 1982 joint communique on arms sales to Taiwan. Those crises were played out within the administration and Republican Party circles. Supporters of Taiwan in Congress played an important role if they were connected with the White House or the Republican Party leadership, but debate over policy never turned the administration against the Congress, as had been the case in the Carter administration.

The shift in Reagan administration policy ultimately came from PRC pressure. From 1980 to 1982, the PRC had gradually become more critical of U.S. China policy as part of the PRC's more indepen-dent position in international affairs. Beijing had apparently believed President Reagan's strong public statements in support of Taiwan at the start of his administration. Moreover, when the PRC began its more independent foreign policy and adopted a tough line toward the United States, its leaders hoped that the United States would become more supportive of PRC interests regarding Taiwan. Beijing almost certainly recognized that it risked alienating the United States, which had served as a vital counterweight for protecting China's security against the USSR for over a decade and had begun to assist China's recent economic development policies. But the PRC seemed to have believed that their room for maneuvering had increased because (1) the United States, under President Reagan's defense buildup, had restored a balance in East-West relations that could check possible Soviet expansion; (2) the Soviet ability to pressure China appeared to be at least temporarily blocked by U.S. power as well as by Soviet domestic and international problems; and (3) at least some important U.S. leaders continued to place a high strategic value on preserving good U.S. relations with China as an important element in U.S. ef-forts to confront and contain Soviet expansion.

Reassessing U.S.-China Relations, 1983–1984

By mid 1983, China's leaders realized that these calculations were mistaken.[15] The United States had adopted a new posture that pub-licly downgraded China's strategic importance to the United States. The change in the U.S. position occurred after the resignation of Sec-retary of State Alexander Haig, perhaps the highest official urging the Reagan administration to sustain good relations with China because it could counter the USSR. Secretary of State George Shultz and his new assistant secretary for East Asian affairs, Paul Wolfowitz, were less supportive of this approach. Shultz held a series of meetings with government and nongovernment Asian specialists in Washington early in 1983 to review U.S. Asian policy in general and policy toward China in particular. The results of his reassessment—to downgrade China's importance to the United States—were reflected in speeches by Shultz and Wolfowitz later in the year.

Administration officials now appeared to judge that efforts to im-prove relations with China were less important than in the recent past because:

- China seemed unlikely to cooperate further with the United

States (through military sales, security consultations, and other matters) against the Soviet Union at a time when the PRC had publicly distanced itself from the United States and had reopened talks on normalization of relations with the USSR.

- China's continued preoccupation with economic modernization made it appear unlikely that the PRC would revert to a highly disruptive position in East Asia that would adversely affect U.S. interests in the stability of the region.
- China's demands on Taiwan, its other bilateral disputes, and accompanying threats to downgrade U.S.-China relations if its demands were not met appeared excessive. These demands had caused a negative reaction in the United States, especially among President Reagan's conservative constituency in Congress and elsewhere; these demands had little support in the United States.
- The United States's ability to deal militarily and politically with the USSR had improved, particularly as a result of the large-scale Reagan administration military budget increases, and there were now serious internal and international difficulties for the USSR.
- United States allies, for the first time in years, were working more closely with Washington in dealing with the Soviet military threat. This was notably true in Asia, where Japanese Prime Minister Nakasone took positions and initiatives strengthening Japanese-U.S. concerns against the Soviet threat.
- Japan and U.S. allies and friends in Southeast Asia appeared more important to the United States for protecting the primary U.S. strategic concerns in the region—safeguarding air and sea access to East Asia, the Indian Ocean, and the Persian Gulf from Soviet attack. By contrast, China did not appear strong enough to cope with this Soviet threat.

Western press reports, quoting authoritative sources in Washington, alerted China to this shift in the U.S. assessment of the PRC's strategic importance. In effect, the U.S. shift meant that China's ability to exploit U.S. interests in strategic relations with China, especially to force the United States to meet China's demands on Taiwan and other questions, had been sharply reduced. At the same time, there was the continued unwillingness of the United States during this period to accede to high-level PRC pressure over Taiwan. The United

States implemented the TRA, granted asylum to Hu Na, and ignored China's demand that Taiwan be thrown out of the Asian Development Bank. The Reagan administration adhered to its principles and waited for Beijing to decide whether to retaliate or to threaten to downgrade relations by withdrawing its ambassador from Washington or to take some other action. Its position received general support in Congress.

Moreover, Beijing began to realize that its political leverage in the United States was weak. The Chinese press noted the strong revival in the U.S. economy in 1983 and the widespread support for President Reagan's re-election. China also must have learned from contact with leading Democrats, notably House Speaker Thomas ("Tip") O'Neill during a visit to China in March 1983, that Beijing could expect little change in U.S. policy toward Taiwan under a Democratic administration. As 1983 wore on, the Chinese began to see an alarming rise in the influence of advocates of self-determination for Taiwan among liberal Democrats. In particular, Senator Claiborne Pell took the lead in passing a controversial resolution in the Senate Foreign Relations Committee that endorsed, among other things, the principles of self-determination for Taiwan.

Although Sino-Soviet trade and cultural and technical contacts increased, Beijing saw little sign of any Soviet willingness to compromise on basic political and security problems for both countries during the talks begun in October 1982. Moreover, the Soviet military buildup in Asia continued unabated, including the deployment of highly accurate SS-20 intermediate-range missiles.

In short, Beijing faced the prospect of a prolonged decline in PRC-U.S. relations, possibly lasting until the end of President Reagan's second term, if it continued to follow the hard line of the previous two years in relations with the United States. Such worsening of relations threatened the implicit but vitally important Chinese strategic consensus with the United States of a prolonged danger posed by the USSR.

Meanwhile, the PRC also recognized that a substantial decline in relations with the United States would have undercut their already limited leverage with Moscow. That worsening of ties would likely have reduced substantially any possible Soviet interest in accommodating China in order to preclude closer U.S.-PRC security ties or collaboration against the USSR. Moreover, China might not be able to gain greater access to U.S. or other capitalist markets and financial and technical assistance and expertise. The Chinese economy was just successfully emerging from the strict readjustments begun in 1980–1981, and the Western economic connection appeared very important to PRC planners. Many U.S. allies and friends, notably Japan, however, were growing reluctant to become heavily involved in China economically at a time of uncertain U.S.-PRC political relations. The United States also exerted strong influence in international financial institutions that were expected to be the source of several billion dollars in aid for China in the 1980s.

China's leaders calculated as well that a serious decline in U.S.-PRC relations would likely result in a concurrent strengthening of U.S.-Taiwan ties. As a result, Beijing's chances of using Taiwan's isolation to prompt Taipei to move toward reunification in accord with PRC interests would be set back seriously.

For all these reasons, then, Beijing began to respond differently and more positively to Reagan administration efforts to ease technology transfer restrictions regarding trade with China, announced by Commerce Secretary Malcolm Baldrige during a trip to China in May 1983. China's leaders followed up by agreeing to schedule a long-delayed visit by Secretary of Defense Caspar Weinberger in September and to exchange visits by Premier Chao and President Reagan at the turn of the year. Beijing media naturally attempted to portray these moves as Chinese responses to U.S. concessions and as being consistent with China's avowed "independent" approach to foreign affairs and its firm stance on U.S.-Taiwan relations. But as time went on, it became transparently clear just how far Beijing was prepared to moderate past public demands and threats of retaliation over Taiwan and other issues for the sake of consolidating U.S.-PRC political, economic, and security ties:

- In 1981, Beijing had publicly disavowed any interest in military purchases from the United States until the United States satisfied China's position on the sale of arms to Taiwan. Beijing noted its dissatisfaction with U.S. arms transfers to Taiwan, which continued at a pace of over $700 million a year, but it now was willing to negotiate purchases of U.S. military equipment with the United States.
- Beijing soft-pedaled past demands, threats, and accusations that the United States was not fulfilling the 1979 and 1982 Sino-U.S. joint communiques.
- Beijing backed away from previous demands that the United States must repeal or amend the TRA or face a decline in relations.
- Beijing muffled previous demands that the United States alter

its position regarding Taiwan's continued membership in the
Asian Development Bank.

- Beijing reduced past criticism of official and unofficial U.S.
contacts with their Taiwan counterparts. It notably avoided
past criticism of U.S. officials being present at Taipei-
sponsored functions in Washington. Beijing was even willing
to turn a blind eye to the almost thirty members of Congress
who traveled to Taiwan in various delegations in January
1984, coinciding with Chao Tzu-yang's trip to Washington.
Beijing even welcomed some of the members who traveled to
the mainland after visiting Taiwan.
- Beijing allowed Northwest Airlines to open services to China
in 1984, even though the airline still served Taiwan. This
marked a contrast from the authoritative Chinese position
adopted in 1983 to oppose Pan American's decision to re-enter
the Taiwan market while also serving the mainland.
- China reduced complaints about the slowness of U.S. technical
transfers to China and about the continued inability of the administration to successfully push legislative changes that
would have allowed the PRC to receive U.S. assistance.

China's greatest compromise was to welcome warmly President
Reagan, in spite of his continued avowed determination to maintain
close U.S. ties with "old friends" in Taiwan and the emphasis of several speeches he delivered in China on the virtues of free speech and
free movement! Beijing was almost certainly well aware that the timing of the visit would serve to assist the president's re-election in the
fall, but it was also aware that the president was unlikely to accommodate PRC interests over Taiwan and some other sensitive issues
during the visit. Indeed, China's news reporting made it clear that
there was no change in the president's position on the Taiwan issue
and implementation of the TRA during the visit. Thus, the best the
Chinese could have hoped for in this regard was to try to consolidate
U.S.-PRC relations to secure broader strategic and economic interests
while possibly expecting that such a closer relationship with time
would reduce the president's firm position toward Taiwan and other
bilateral disputes.

The Reagan administration, meanwhile, attempted to improve the
relationship by accommodating PRC concerns through the avoidance
of strong rhetorical support for Taiwan, which in the past had so in-
flamed U.S.-PRC tensions, and by moving ahead on military and
technology transfers to the PRC. Nevertheless, when the U.S.-PRC

nuclear cooperation agreement, which had been initiated during the president's visit, became stalled because of opposition from nonproliferation advocates in the United States who were concerned about reports of China's support for Pakistan's alleged nuclear weapons program, China went along with administration explanations with only minor complaint. In short, it appeared that Beijing was determined to further strengthen military and economic ties with the United States and to soft-pedal bilateral difficulties. On the Taiwan issue, Beijing retreated to a baseline position that asked for U.S. adherence to the joint communiqués and accelerated reduction of U.S. arms sales to Taiwan, but the PRC was not prepared to make a significant issue of the question unless egregiously provoked.

The New Consensus
Over China Policy

Members of Congress generally supported the results of the reassessment of U.S. China policy in 1982–1983, which saw a decline in U.S. policy makers' concern over the U.S. position in the U.S.-PRC-Taiwan and the U.S.-PRC-Soviet triangular relationships. Congress also showed less interest in issues involving implementing the TRA. A consensus finally emerged among policy makers in both branches of government that the existing TRA framework provided an effective means for handling U.S.-Taiwan issues, such as trade, human rights, and immigration. Political and military issues relating directly to the U.S.-PRC-Taiwan triangular relationship remained sensitive, such as U.S. arms sales to Taiwan and the mainland, Taiwan's position in international bodies like the Asian Development Bank, and efforts by some in Taiwan and the United States to foster self-determination for the people on Taiwan. Congress and the executive branch had now developed effective consultative mechanisms to deal with these issues. Their differences had narrowed as the United States, the PRC, and Taiwan now realized that their interests had been largely achieved, at least for the present, by the working arrangements under the TRA.

Few members of Congress worried about a review of how the TRA was being implemented. Congressional concerns had shifted to such issues as the growing U.S. trade deficit and economic disputes with Taiwan, human rights, and the prospects for democracy after martial law ended in 1987 and President Chiang Ching-kuo died in

January 1988. Yet, U.S. officials in the Congress and the administration managed to deal effectively with these issues through the mechanisms established under the broad framework of the TRA. Policy actions toward Taiwan in these economic and human rights areas were markedly similar to those taken by both branches of the U.S. government to handle the same issues in U.S. relations with South Korea and other countries.

The question of U.S. arms sales to Taiwan and the PRC remained one of the most sensitive questions regarding the implementation of the TRA. But Congress had accepted the balance in U.S. policy, based on roughly $700 million worth of U.S. military equipment and technology being transferred annually to Taiwan and a much more modest U.S. program of military exchanges with the PRC.

Recently, broad congressional support for greater democracy and human rights in Taiwan (a major concern in the TRA) has involved the efforts of some members to back strongly those in Taiwan and abroad who demand that the people on Taiwan have the right to determine the future political status of the island. (A notable group in the United States that is advocating self-determination for Taiwan is the Formosan Association for Public Affairs, which has been effective in getting its message to many members of Congress and their staffs.) These congressional efforts must take into account both Beijing and Taipei's worry that Taiwan's de jure independence from the mainland will gain great momentum. Both the Chinese Communists and the Nationalists oppose such a movement. Up to this time, neither the administration nor the Congress, with a few exceptions, has wanted to support such a movement and disrupt U.S. relations with Beijing and Taipei.

Without formal congressional review or explicit attention to the implementation of the TRA, some observers have speculated that Congress might be less supportive of the law and its requirements.[16] They argue that support for the TRA is now in the hands of the executive branch, whose China policy could change and adversely influence Taiwan and U.S. interest in the Pacific Basin. These observers sometimes call for the U.S. Congress to be more active in implementing the TRA. In their view, Congress needs to establish some enforcement mechanisms and institutionalize the way the United States now implements the TRA to strengthen the foundations of future U.S.-Taiwan relations.

Yet other observers insist that, unless some crisis erupts over Taiwan, Congress is unlikely to review the TRA in order to establish new oversight or enforcement mechanisms. Members are simply too preoccupied with other issues to devote much time to "fix something that isn't broken." They recognize that the TRA has few enforcement mechanisms at present, but Congress relies on close consultations between the administration and concerned congressional members and staff within the TRA framework to handle any difficult political or military issues that might arise. Such consultation works much better now than it did in the early years of the TRA because there is less secrecy and freer interchange over policy among officials of the two branches. Meanwhile, less politically sensitive issues in U.S.-Taiwan relations are expeditiously handled under the routine mechanisms already established by the TRA.

The absence of a more institutionalized framework for implementing the TRA does not mean that support in Congress for the law has weakened. Congressional support for strong ties with Taiwan and the implementation of the TRA comes from several quarters and is based on several factors: (1) Taiwan's growing economic importance to the United States and its new power in international finance, (2) strong and effective Taiwan government efforts to familiarize the members of Congress and their staffs with Taipei's needs for a strong implementation of the TRA, and (3) traditional congressional concern to maintain, through the TRA, the special influence that Congress exerts over U.S. policy toward Taiwan.

Under these circumstances, those in Taiwan and elsewhere who worry about the absence of any institutions to enforce the TRA should rest assured that the political support for the TRA is very likely to remain strong in Congress. Although such support for the TRA is not expressed explicitly when Congress agrees with the U.S. policy toward Taiwan, Congress can be expected to respond strongly to protect its prerogatives under the TRA and safeguard Taiwan's interests in the event that a future administration shifts its policy.

Notes

1. For background on U.S.-PRC-ROC relations during the Carter and Reagan administrations, see Zbigniew Brzezinski, *Power and Principle: Memoirs of the National Security Advisor, 1977–1981* (New York: Farrar, Straus & Giroux, 1983), chapter 6 (pp. 196–233) and chapter 11 (pp. 403–25); Michel Oksenberg, "A Decade of Sino-American Relations," *Foreign Affairs* 61, no. 1 (Fall 1982): 175–95; A. Doak Barnett, *U.S. Arms Sales: The China-Taiwan Tangle* (Washington, D.C.: Brookings Institution, 1982); George R. Packard, "Policy Paper," in *Report of the Atlantic Council's Committee on China Policy* (Boston: Oelgeschlager, Gunn & Hain, 1984), pp. 1–46; Cyrus Vance, *Hard*

Choices (New York: Simon & Schuster, 1983), chapters 2 and 3 (pp. 26–35, 45–46, 75–83, and 113–19); Harold Brown, *Thinking About Foreign Policy* (Boulder, Colo.: Westview Press, 1983), chapter 7 (pp. 113–40); Jimmy Carter, *Keeping Faith* (New York: Bantam Books, 1982), pp. 186–211; Alexander Haig, Jr., *Caveat: Realism, Reagan, and Foreign Policy* (New York: Macmillan, 1984), pp. 194–217; Michel Oksenberg, "China Policy for the 1980s," *Foreign Affairs* 59, no. 2 (Winter/Spring 1981–82): 304–22; A. Doak Barnett, *The FX Decision* (Washington, D.C.: Brookings Institution, 1981); Huan Hsiang, "On Sino-American Relations," *Foreign Affairs* 60, no. 1 (1981): 34–53; Jaw-ling Joanne Chang, *Peking's Negotiating Style: A Case Study of U.S.-PRC Normalization* Occasional Papers in Contemporary Asian Studies, no. 5 (Baltimore: Maryland School of Law, 1985); Robert Downen, *The Taiwan Pawn in the China Game* (Washington, D.C.: Center for Strategic and International Studies, 1979); Martin Lasater, *The Taiwan Issue in Sino-American Strategic Relations* (Boulder, Colo.: Westview Press, 1984); Jonathan Pollack, *The Lessons of Coalition Politics: Sino-American Security Relations* (Santa Monica, Calif.: Rand Corporation, 1984); U. Alexis Johnson (ed.), *China: Policy for the Next Decade* (Boston: Oelgeschlager, Gunn & Hain, 1984).

2. U.S. Department of State, Bureau of Public Affairs, *U.S. Policy Toward China, July 15, 1971–January 15, 1979: Selected Documents, No. 9* (Washington, D.C.: Government Printing Office, 1979).

3. U.S. Congress, *Taiwan Enabling Act, March 1979* (Washington, D.C.: Government Printing Office, 1979), pp. 61–63.

4. Ibid., pp. 7–8.

5. Ibid., p. 7.

6. U.S. Congress, *Taiwan Hearings* (Washington, D.C.: Government Printing Office, 1979), pp. 51–52.

7. U.S. Congress, *Taiwan Legislation: Hearings* (Washington, D.C.: Government Printing Office, 1980), p. 113.

8. *New York Times*, February 13, 1979.

9. U.S. Congress, *Taiwan Enabling Act*, p. 4.

10. Ibid., pp. 20–22.

11. U.S. Congress, *Implementation of the Taiwan Relations Act: Hearings* (Washington, D.C.: Government Printing Office, 1979), p. 37.

12. For background on the interviews noted here and later in this article, see Robert G. Sutter, *The China Quandary: Domestic Determinants of U.S. China Policy, 1972–1982* (Boulder, Colo.: Westview Press, 1983), pp. 89–110.

13. Ibid.

14. For background, see U.S. Library of Congress, Congressional Research Service, *Trip Report on Visit to Taiwan, August 13–19, 1986 [by] Robert G. Sutter, August 25, 1986*, (n.p., n.d.).

15. For background, see Pollack, *The Lessons of Coalition Politics*; Robert G. Sutter, *Chinese Foreign Policy: Developments After Mao* (New York: Praeger, 1986), pp. 176–86.

16. These observations, drawn from many years observing debates over the TRA in Washington, D.C., were reinforced as a result of listening to deliberations held at the Hoover Institution on September 10, 1988 in conjunction with the preparation of this book.

RICHARD BUSH

Helping the Republic of China to Defend Itself

THE SECURITY SECTION of the Taiwan Relations Act (TRA), especially the part relating to arms transfer, is among the most prominent examples of Congress's post-Vietnam struggle to carve out a larger role in the formulation of foreign policy.[1] Members of Congress on both sides of the aisle, angered by a presidential decision made with a perceived absence of interbranch consultation, sought through legislation to ensure that a friend and former ally had the means to defend itself.[2]

Tempers have cooled since the stormy days that followed the normalization of U.S.-PRC relations, and fears about Taiwan's future have never materialized. The passage of time now permits a dispassionate analysis of how well the security provisions of the TRA have worked, both as a means of ensuring peace and stability in the Taiwan Strait and as a congressional attempt to influence U.S. foreign policy.

To evaluate the arms transfer provisions of the TRA, we need to consider the following issues in order to learn to what extent the Republic of China (ROC) has been able to depend on the TRA in maintaining its security:

1. What part did arms sales to the ROC play in the negotiations over the normalization of U.S.-PRC relations?

The views expressed in this essay are those of the author and not necessarily those of the House Foreign Affairs Committee or any of its Members.

2. What is the meaning of the arms sales provision as law?

3. What complications were introduced in arms shipments to Taiwan by the U.S.-PRC communiqué of August 17, 1982?

4. How have the arms sales provisions been implemented with respect to process and substance?

5. How successful has the ROC been in moving toward "import substitution" in weapons acquisition?

6. What has been the effect of U.S. arms sales to China on Taiwan arms transfer policy?

7. What are the prospects for the future?

Arms Sales to the ROC as an Issue in U.S.-PRC Normalization

How was the issue of U.S. arms transfers to the ROC handled during the U.S. negotiations with the PRC over the normalization of diplomatic relations? Four key participants have left memoirs, which, taken together, provide clear outlines of the bilateral discussions.[3]

That this issue remains a source of dispute with the PRC should be no surprise. Anything that keeps the United States involved in the Chinese civil war always raises some objections in Beijing. What, in retrospect, is passing strange is that Beijing did not make more of an effort to secure an end to U.S. arms transfers to Taipei. The PRC's preferences were clear from the beginning: Li Hsien-nien said in October 1977 that it would be "inappropriate" for the ROC to receive U.S. weapons after normalization.[4] But arms transfer was not on the PRC's list of nonnegotiable conditions for normalization, as were derecognition of the Taipei government, repudiation of the 1954 mutual defense treaty, and the withdrawal of all U.S. military forces from Taiwan.

Could the omission have been intentional? The PRC's leaders surely remembered the massive stocks of military equipment that the United States left to the Nationalist forces during the late 1940s and the military and psychological lift that aid gave to sagging Kuomintang fortunes. In the late 1970s, arms transfers were unquestionably more important militarily to the ROC's security than were U.S. forces, on whose withdrawal the PRC did insist. Yet with the United

States apparently ready to cut back its security ties with the ROC, why did Beijing not push harder to sever that last umbilical cord? We may never know.

For its part, the Carter administration made an early decision, for moral and political reasons, to set security conditions of its own before normalizing relations with Beijing. As early as June 1977, President Carter decided that, unless the United States could continue arms sales to the ROC, and unless the PRC accepted a unilateral U.S. resolution demanding peaceful settlement of the Taiwan issue, he would not go forward with normalization.[5]

These conditions were included in the instructions to Cyrus Vance when he journeyed to the PRC in August 1977, and in those of Zbigniew Brzezinski when he went in May 1978.[6] They were part of the negotiating instructions conveyed to Leonard Woodcock, the U.S. Liaison Office head in Beijing, for the talks he began with Chinese officials in June 1978.[7] They were also reiterated in a key meeting on September 19, 1978, between President Carter and Ch'ai Tze-min, the head of the PRC Liaison Office in Washington. Brzezinski reports that Carter "made a very effective statement of our policy to China and hit the Chinese hard on our right to sell arms to Taiwan and on the importance of a noncontradicted statement by the United States to the effect that we expected a peaceful resolution of the issue of Taiwan."[8]

The memoirs suggest, however, that the arms sale issue was not addressed explicitly in Beijing until very late in the game. Neither Vance nor Brzezinski raised it during their visits.[9] Woodcock was instructed not to raise the subject until the success of the negotiations was fairly certain. Indeed, it was not until Teng Hsiao-p'ing became his interlocutor on December 13 that the arms sale issue was raised. It is true that President Carter had discussed arms sales with Ch'ai Tze-min in September, yet, for reasons that have yet to be explained, Woodcock's counterparts in the Foreign Ministry reportedly chose not to take up the matter.[10]

This reticence is even more mysterious, given the lack of specificity with which U.S. officials raised the U.S.-ROC security relationship in general and arms sales in particular. Brzezinski told Teng Hsiao-p'ing in May 1978 "that our security commitment to Taiwan would continue even after normalization, during the 'historically transitional era' (a deliberately vague phrase that I used to describe Taiwan's continued separate status, prior to some eventual reunification.)"[11] Woodcock's negotiating instructions referred only to "selective arms sales for defensive purposes."[12] And in his September conversation with Ch'ai Tze-min, Carter used the formulation "carefully selected arms sales to Taiwan that would not be threatening to China."[13]

Whatever the reason for Beijing's avoidance of the issue of Taiwan arms sales, normalization almost foundered on it. Teng and Woodcock reached a basic normalization agreement on December 13, and Teng sought only a suspension of arms transfers during the one year during which the mutual defense treaty was being terminated. The next day, however, the Chinese apparently sought to withdraw the concession. Brzezinski's diary for the 15th says: "Unfortunately, at the last minute [on the 14th] the arms sales issue has arisen. The Chinese are operating on the assumption that we will discontinue immediately."[14]

In the end, it was only possible to agree to disagree. In another Teng-Woodcock meeting, the two sides stated positions that were clearly in conflict. Oksenberg records, "The president's formulation of September 19 was repeated. The Chinese responded in equally firm fashion that arms sales to Taiwan infringed on Chinese sovereignty and could not be accepted."[15] Brzezinski writes that Woodcock was instructed to say that the United States would be restrained on the issue but that the realities of U.S. politics required that the U.S. government at least be prepared, when the inevitable question came, to reaffirm that weapons transfers to Taiwan would continue. Woodcock told Teng that the United States would say publicly that "the Chinese side does not endorse the United States position on this matter, but it has not prevented both sides from agreeing to normalize relations."[16]

Oksenberg sums up the Carter administration's view of where the issue was left:

> Hence the negotiating record is clear. No agreement was reached on this most difficult issue. In agreeing to normalize relations, the two sides deferred their differences on continued U.S. arms sales to Taiwan. The Chinese reserved the right to raise the issue again, and American officials expressed the belief that the post-normalization era would gradually offer a better environment for discussing the issue. The United States at no point placed a time limit on these sales or pledged to curtail them over time. Nonetheless, implicit in the American position was that the quantity and quality of sales would be linked to Beijing's position on Taiwan.[17]

A possible explanation for the reversal of Beijing's position is that Teng Hsiao-p'ing and the other Chinese officials directly involved in the negotiations were unable to sell the initial agreement to others in the leadership. If so, these opponents of the deal had a perspective analogous to that of the U.S. Congress vis-à-vis the executive branch. Distressed at not being consulted on normalization, many members of Congress would seek to remedy through legislation what they perceived to be the deficiencies of the bargain. What they may not have known was that the arms transfer issue was unfinished business.

The Security Provisions of the Taiwan Relations Act

The security section of the TRA contains the following policy statement in Section 2(b):

> (b) It is the policy of the United States: . . . (2) to declare that peace and stability in the [Western Pacific] area are in the political, security, and economic interests of the United States, and are matters of international concern;
> (3) to make clear that the United States' decision to establish diplomatic relations with the People's Republic of China rests on the expectation that the future of Taiwan will be determined by peaceful means;
> (4) to consider any effort to determine the future of Taiwan by other than peaceful means, including by boycotts or embargoes, a threat to the peace and security of the Western Pacific area and of grave concern to the United States;
> (5) to provide Taiwan with arms of a defensive character;
> (6) to maintain the capacity of the United States to resist any resort to force or other forms of coercion that would jeopardize the security, or the social or economic system, of the people on Taiwan.[18]

For the most part, these policy statements are consistent with the Carter administration's approach to normalization with Beijing. Subsections 3 and 5 conform to its two conditions. Subsection 4 merely makes explicit what was implicit in the administration's statement of expectation of a peaceful solution. Subsection 6, however, goes beyond the executive branch's position. It can be seen both as an analogue to the abrogated security treaty and as a response by the Congress to the Chinese refusal to give up the right to use force against Taiwan, even in the context of statements of peaceful intentions. This U.S. pledge of support, however, is phrased in terms of capabilities only, not intentions.

Sections 3(a) and 3(b) of the Act set forth the implementing provision on arms transfers, as follows:

> (a) In furtherance of the policy set forth in section 2 of this Act, the United States will make available to Taiwan such defense articles and defense services in such quantity as may be necessary to enable Taiwan to maintain a sufficient self-defense capability.
>
> (b) The President and the Congress shall determine the nature and quantity of such defense articles and services based solely upon their judgment of the needs of Taiwan, in accordance with the procedures established by law. Such determination of Taiwan's defense needs shall include review by United States' military authorities in connection with recommendations to the President and the Congress.[19]

The policy and implementation provisions are interesting in several respects. One question concerns the status of statements of policy in a piece of legislation. In this case, does Section 2 of the TRA have any binding effect? In part, the answer is a function of one's views on the constitutional powers of the president to conduct foreign policy. Those who favor the congressional role in foreign affairs place greater value on such legislated statements of policy than do defenders of executive branch authority. In addition, it makes a difference whether the policies included in a law are expressed as statements of fact or as prescriptions for administration action. In the case of the TRA, the use of the verb *is* in the clause "It is the policy of the United States . . . " indicates that what follows has no binding force.[20]

Second, and similarly, the first part of the implementing provision of the TRA contains less than meets the eye. In U.S. legislative practice, the Congress requires an action by the executive through the use of the word *shall*. To say that "the United States will make available to Taiwan such defense articles and defense services . . . " represents less a mandate for action than a statement of intention.[21]

Third, there is an ambiguity as to what precisely the United States should provide Taiwan. The policy statement in Section 2(b)(5) of the TRA and the Carter administration's pledges to Beijing refer to defensive weapons. Section 3(a) of the TRA speaks of defense articles that ensure a self-defense capability for Taiwan. Yet if the island were attacked, the most effective defense would probably be attacks by the Nationalist Air Force on air and naval bases on the Chinese mainland, which would require weapons of an offensive character.

Fourth, the requirement that U.S. government decisions on arms sales to Taiwan be based solely on the executive-congressional judgment of the needs of Taiwan was written to exclude a PRC voice in such decisions. Indeed, the House version of the bill specifically rules out consideration of PRC views. That reference was removed in the House-Senate conference on the TRA, but Representative Edward Derwinski, in commenting on the action of the conference committee, indicated that the intent of Section 3(b) remained the same as the House provision.[22] However, what Congress may have forgotten—or not known in the first place—was that Beijing, with U.S. consent, had reserved the right to reopen the arms transfer issue. Consequently, this provision was in potential jeopardy from the moment it was enacted.

Fifth, there is no indication either in the legislation itself or in the accompanying documents and statements (the legislative history) as to how the U.S. government should go about deciding, in a substantive sense, what Taiwan's needs are. Obviously, U.S. obligations to Taiwan would vary tremendously, depending on the criteria used to gauge its requirements. For example, the U.S. judgment might be based on PRC intentions, on PRC capabilities, or on both. Similarly, what Washington is willing to provide will vary according to how much weaponry it expects Taiwan to produce on its own and purchase elsewhere.

At the time that Congress was drafting the TRA, many wanted the legislation to state explicitly what the United States should supply to the ROC. According to the late Senator Jacob Javits, key members of the House and Senate, angered by the minimal reference to arms transfers in the administration's draft bill, advocated "provisions that would . . . have committed the United States to automatic large-scale transfer of military equipment."[23] In the end, that was not done, and how Taiwan's needs were to be defined was never clarified.

Finally, there is an ambiguity in the arms transfer provision of the TRA about the respective roles of the executive and legislative branches in decision making. The wording "the president and the Congress shall determine" weapons transfers to the ROC suggests a greater than normal congressional role. At a House Foreign Affairs Committee hearing on November 8, 1979, Congressman Robert Lagomarsino told Deputy Secretary of State Warren Christopher, "As the [TRA] states . . . this body and specifically this committee take a direct interest in the nature and quantity of arms sold to Taiwan and intend to be a full partner in any decision made on this matter."[24]

However, the statement "the president and the Congress shall determine" is balanced—and probably negated—by the phrase "in accordance with the procedures established by law."[25] Interviews with congressional staff members who worked on the TRA indicate that they do not recall any effort to establish extraordinary procedures for the ROC. Moreover, a General Accounting Office report on the TRA concluded that the act "as written does not give the Congress a voice in determining Taiwan's defensive arms needs earlier in the decision-making process" than otherwise required by law.[26]

In short, the TRA does not mandate the sale of arms to the ROC because it is not self-enforcing in either a substantive or a procedural sense. In drafting the TRA, the Congress failed to make clear the meaning of the phrase "necessary to enable Taiwan to maintain a sufficient self-defense capability" and failed to specify how the Congress was to be a decision-making partner with the executive. Having passed a law granting the administration decision-making authority, Congress would have to assert itself politically if it wished to influence what defense equipment the ROC received.

Indeed, even when President Carter reluctantly signed the TRA, he interpreted the new law to emphasize what Congress had not done, and so he buttressed the prerogatives of the executive branch. He commented:

> The act contains all of the authority that I requested in order to enable us to maintain [commercial, cultural and other—read "arms sales"] unofficial relations with the people on Taiwan . . . In a number of sections of this legislation, the Congress has wisely granted discretion to the president. In all instances, I will exercise that discretion in a manner consistent with our interest in the well-being of the people on Taiwan, and with the understanding we reached on the normalization of relations with the People's Republic of China . . . [27]

According to one Carter administration official, the president claimed that the TRA empowered him to do what he felt was appropriate vis-à-vis Taiwan and bound him in no significant way.[28]

The August 17, 1982 Communiqué

Ronald Reagan's nomination as the Republican Party's 1980 presidential candidate marked a serious deterioration in the U.S.-PRC relationship. By October 1981, Beijing reopened the arms sale issue, which was not closed until August 17, 1982, with a new joint communiqué that raised questions about the TRA's integrity and introduced more problems for its implementation.[29]

Early in the Reagan administration, PRC officials warned their U.S. counterparts that providing arms for the ROC was a sensitive question and that there was a limit to their tolerance.[30] By the fall of 1981, the Chinese declared that their patience was exhausted. In October, Foreign Minister Huang Hua proposed in a Washington meeting with Secretary of State Alexander Haig that the United States not exceed the level of sales in the Carter years, that it reduce that level year by year, and that it set a date for termination of the transfers.[31]

Negotiations began in December, and the two sides went through many drafts before reaching final agreement. Haig's memoirs and the communiqué suggest that the Reagan administration was prepared from the outset to meet the Chinese demand on quantitative limits because the level of recent arms sales provided a high base from which to make any reductions.[32] The administration's decision not to sell the FX aircraft to Taiwan, which was communicated to Beijing in January 1982, may have signaled its willingness to accept qualitative limits.

The key sticking point appears to have been whether the administration would set a date for ending arms sales. Even Haig, committed as he was to strengthening the PRC relationship, knew that the United States would not concede that point. When Huang Hua had made his original request, Haig angrily replied that such a demand placed an intolerable burden on the relationship.[33] In his memoirs, Haig hints that someone—presumably the Chinese—suggested a secret agreement on a terminal date. His advice to the president just before he left the administration was to reject that proposal: "Any understanding with the Chinese on this issue had to be made public; secret agreements cannot be defended before the public and the Congress."[34]

Both sides also found it necessary to create the political will to cut a deal. For the Chinese, that seems to have occurred in May 1982, when Vice-President Bush reiterated in Beijing the Carter administration commitment that "the Taiwan Relations Act could and would be administered in a way consistent with the normalization communiqué." Haig reports that Teng had decided at that point to settle because he believed China would get no more concessions from the United States.[35]

In the United States, administration officials had to convince President Reagan, now under fire from his conservative friends, that the pending agreement would allow him to preserve the PRC relationship without undercutting his strong commitment to the ROC. Near the end of his tour as secretary of state, Haig used his meager political capital in one last effort to persuade the president. He reminded

Reagan that his objectives were "to preserve the strategic relationship with China, to preserve American honor, and to assure the continuing well-being of the people of Taiwan through a settlement that permitted arms sales to Taiwan with future reductions tied to China's peaceful approach to reunion with Taiwan." President Reagan finally agreed.[36]

Thus, a new compromise was reached. The key section of the August 17, 1982 communiqué, a more complete version of which appears as Appendix A, reads as follows:

> 6. Having in mind the foregoing statements of both sides, the United States Government states that it does not seek to carry out a long-term policy of arms sales to Taiwan, that its arms sales to Taiwan will not exceed, either in qualitative or in quantitative terms, the level of those supplied in recent years since the establishment of diplomatic relations between the United States and China, and that it intends to reduce gradually its sales of arms to Taiwan, leading over a period of time to a final resolution.

To justify these commitments, the Reagan administration emphasized the PRC's willingness to settle the Taiwan question peacefully. The communiqué referred three times to China's "fundamental policy of striving for a peaceful solution to the Taiwan question" and cited as support of this goal the National People's Congress Standing Committee's statement of January 1, 1979, and Yeh Chien-ying's nine-point proposal of September 30, 1981. Yet the PRC remained unwilling to renounce the use of force with respect to Taiwan. Did this new PRC formulation represent a significant departure from its approach at the time of normalization—its willingness to negotiate "peaceful reunification" and its silence regarding the U.S. demand for a peaceful solution?

If the communiqué's objective was to put the arms sale issue to rest, it probably failed. When the communiqué was issued, both the PRC and U.S. governments issued statements that gave conflicting interpretations of the document. Among the points of disagreement were the following issues:

The basis of U.S. reduction of arms sales to Taiwan. The PRC statement asserted that the arms sales issue was governed by the principles of respect for each other's sovereignty and territorial integrity and noninterference in each other's internal affairs, that the communiqué had reaffirmed these principles, and that they "emphatically" would "continue to govern all aspects of their relations." Furthermore, the Chinese side asserted that its policy of peaceful reunification was an "internal affair" and that "no misinterpretation or foreign interference is permissible."[37]

President Reagan's statement said, "Arms sales will continue . . . with the full expectation that the approach of the Chinese government to the resolution of the Taiwan issue will continue to be peaceful. We attach great significance to the Chinese statement in the communiqué regarding China's 'fundamental' policy; and it is clear from our statements that our future actions will be conducted with this peaceful policy fully in mind."[38]

The meaning of the term "final resolution." The Chinese statement said, "The final resolution referred to here certainly implies that the U.S. arms sales to Taiwan must be completely terminated over a period of time." President Reagan's statement applied the word *resolution* only to the Taiwan issue in general and not to arms sales in particular. Moreover, Assistant Secretary of State John Holdridge told the Senate Foreign Relations Committee that "the statements of future U.S. arms sales policy embodied in the Communiqué do not provide either a time frame for reductions of U.S. arms sales or for their termination."[39]

The relationship of the communiqué to the TRA. The Chinese Foreign Ministry asserted, "All interpretations designed to link the present joint communiqué to the 'Taiwan Relations Act' are in violation of the spirit and substance of this communiqué and are thus unacceptable." President Reagan, however, said: "Regarding future U.S. arms sales to Taiwan, our policy, set forth clearly in the communiqué, is fully consistent with the Taiwan Relations Act. Arms sales will continue in accordance with the Act . . . "[40]

Neither side made clear the terms *quality* or *quantity,* how the baseline for reductions was to be set, the rate at which those reductions were to occur, and when a "final resolution" might come. Congressmen Stephen Solarz and Lee Hamilton raised some of these terms and issues when Holdridge appeared before the House Foreign Affairs Committee, but he never provided clear answers.[41]

Congressional critics of the communiqué focused their ire on what they saw as a violation of the TRA's demands that the PRC play no role in determining U.S. arms sales to the ROC. Some members were especially indignant. Senator John Glenn, chairman of the East Asian and Pacific Affairs Committee when the TRA became law, was particularly blunt:

Along with the chairman and other members of the committee, I helped draft the . . . TRA; so we, better than most perhaps, know what we intended to accomplish in that act. And I can tell you that in my considered judgment the communiqué announced today does undermine the spirit and intent of the TRA. The legislative history demonstrates beyond a doubt that the intent of . . . [Section 3 of the TRA] was to insure that arms sales decisions, albeit prudent and cautious, would be made in Washington, not in Peking or Taipei. Now, because we anticipated the PRC would pressure us to end or limit Taiwan arms sales, we provided in the act a framework for the executive branch to resist such pressures . . . The communiqué announced today discards that very carefully crafted framework, the heart of the TRA, in favor of an arms sales formulation negotiated under Chinese threats of a retrogression of United States-PRC relations.[42]

The administration would have been more embarrassed by these criticisms had it not pledged to the ROC one month earlier that it had not agreed to hold prior consultations with Beijing on arms sales to the ROC.[43]

In 1982 and 1983, the Senate Subcommittee on Separation of Powers held a series of hearings exploring the relationship between the communiqué and the TRA in an effort to determine whether the Reagan administration had exceeded its authority.[44]

The subcommittee, chaired by conservative Senator John East, began its deliberations by displaying suspicion of the administration. In the end, however, it chose to avoid a constitutional crisis with an equally conservative president. After many meetings, the panel finally decided that the communiqué and the TRA were not fundamentally contradictory. Its key conclusions were as follows:

1. The administration has not offered clear and consistent accounts either of the nature of the joint communiqué or of the legal nature of the policy statements made therein.
2. The apparent meaning of the U.S. policy statements in paragraph 6 of the communiqué is inconsistent with the policy set forth in the Taiwan Relations Act.
3. The administration, particularly President Reagan, has repeatedly articulated an interpretation of these policy statements that is generally consistent with the Taiwan Relations Act.[45]

Senator East's subcommittee might have been less willing to square the legal circle had it not been for a decision by the administration in early 1983 to make no more concessions to Beijing. There was now little need for Congress to come to the ROC's defense.[46]

Still, the August 1982 communiqué did not resolve the underlying dispute between the United States and the PRC. The two sides still had serious differences; they had merely refined how they would agree to disagree. From a U.S. perspective, the compromise of 1982, with its specific pledges on quality and quantity, imposed greater constraints than the compromise of 1978. If Washington's later actions were inconsistent with Beijing's interpretation of the communiqué, the PRC could reopen the issue. A September 1982 statement by State Department legal adviser Davis Robinson to East's subcommittee seemed to agree. "Certainly a communiqué of this nature cannot bind any future President of the United States."[47]

Congress's Role in
Arms Sales to Taiwan

How did Congress's limited powers to influence arms transfer policy affect the ROC under the TRA? After World War II, the executive branch had secured broad authority to decide arms sales. In the wake of the Vietnam War, Congress tried to regain some control over those decisions but did not get very far. Currently, the Arms Export Control Act requires only that the executive branch formally notify Congress thirty days before it intends to issue a letter of offer and acceptance for a government-to-government arms sale or to issue a license for a commercial transaction, and only for arms transfer packages worth more than $50 million or for certain major defense equipment items worth more than $14 million. During that month, consultations occasionally occur between administration officials and the committees of jurisdiction—the House Foreign Affairs Committee and the Senate Foreign Relations Committee—and other members. The House and Senate committees may also hold public hearings or closed briefings during the consultation period.

Congress does not have to approve an arms transfer for it to go forward. Theoretically, it has the right to pass legislation forbidding an arms sale. Congress may try to pass a law requiring the administration to make a sale that it does not wish to make. Or Congress may threaten to take such actions.[48] Yet the political will and strength to exercise that option usually exists only on weapons transfers to Arab countries.

Therefore, those in Congress who wish to influence arms sales to the ROC or other parties must rely on political pressure. Individual members or groups of members may act as individual legislators, expressing their views through letters to the president or the secretary of state or through public statements. Or pressure may come from the committees of jurisdiction, which represent the Congress institutionally vis-à-vis the administration. They may hold hearings or briefings on a particular arms transfer or on the broad underlying policy. They may take a formal position on a sale in the form of a letter or public statement. And they may seek broader interbranch consultation than that required by statute in order to have a greater effect on the decisions.

The executive branch makes a calculated judgment on how seriously it should respond to congressional efforts to influence arms sale policy. It may be willing to engage in regular consultation concerning its arms transfer plans with the relevant members of Congress, particularly the chairmen of committees and subcommittees of jurisdiction. Yet these discussions occur only after a consensus on a specific arms sale has been reached within the administration and only if it is believed that they will enhance chances for acceptance.[49] With respect to proposals that come from members speaking for themselves, an administration will give more weight to the pleas of committees and powerful members than to those of members who are in no position to do it any damage. Proposals that are at odds with fundamental administration policy are more likely to be ignored than those that are not, especially if there are those in Congress who actively support the president's position.

In the first few years after U.S.-PRC normalization, there were some congressional efforts both to expand consultation on ROC arms sales in general and to lobby on the sale of an advanced fighter in particular. In retrospect, however, these activities were relatively ineffective and short lived.

In the last year of the Carter administration, there was sharp criticism from Capitol Hill regarding the low level of consultation. At a June 1980 hearing, Lester Wolff, the chairman of the House Asian Affairs Subcommittee, complained of a "serious breakdown" in the interaction between the two branches and charged that Congress was frequently informed of decisions that were "unilateral" and not "made with the input" of Congress. A General Accounting Office (GAO) study commissioned in the spring of 1979 and released in the spring of 1980 cited insufficient congressional involvement in arms sale decisions. A GAO representative testified as follows to the two Asian and Pacific Affairs subcommittees:

> The executive branch to date has made little effort to explain what specific plans there may be for future Taiwan arms sales. The legislative history of the act implies that the Congress expected to be closely consulted about Taiwan's defense needs and U.S. plans to meet them . . . Although the Congress was assured many times by the State Department that close contacts with the Congress would be maintained, the "what" and "when" aspects of consultation regarding . . . military sales could be improved . . . No information was provided to the Congress on what items would be recommended or on what the executive branch's future arms strategy would be even though the Congress was briefed on Taiwan's request for military equipment . . . One of the reasons for absent or inadequate consultation is that the executive branch's decisions . . . on military sales are made and closely held by a small group of top-level U.S. officials.[50]

The Carter administration felt otherwise. At the June 1980 hearing, Assistant Secretary Richard Holbrooke asserted that consultation on Taiwan "has been rather extensive by normal executive-legislative branch standards," that Congress wanted a "level of specificity in regard to Taiwan that exceeds that . . . [for] any other country or area," and that members of Congress were not always available to be consulted.[51]

The level of consultation was not discussed again publicly until the release of the August 1982 communiqué. Here, even congressional judgments were mixed. Senator Charles Percy, chairman of the Senate Foreign Relations Committee, commended executive branch officials for their "forthright and candid approach to the committee" and called the interactions "a model of the consultative process of which both branches . . . can be justifiably proud." Senator Larry Pressler, however, "politely disagreed . . . that this is a model for consultation with Congress in advance of a decision" because of the restrictive ground rules under which discussions took place. Congressman Stephen Solarz, chairman of the House Subcommittee on Asian and Pacific Affairs, was not briefed on the details of the negotiations until right before the communiqué was released, and his office was particularly surprised by the specific limitations on quality and quantity.[52]

Capitol Hill lobbying for the FX fighter began soon after normalization. During 1979 and 1980, both the House and Senate committees informally urged that the ROC be permitted to open discussions with manufacturers of the FX aircraft, and the Carter administration eventually acceded to those requests. Once Ronald Reagan took office, the ROC's friends in Congress supported those in the administration who favored selling an advanced fighter. In contrast, the House Asian Affairs Subcommittee supported Secretary Haig's position in a June 1981 letter to President Reagan. It opposed both the FX aircraft to the ROC and any U.S. weapons to the PRC.[53] Because congressional sentiment was divided, the issue was ultimately determined by the bureaucratic politics within the administration. Once Richard Allen had left his post as National Security Adviser, Haig and others persuaded the president to disregard the FX advocates for the sake of U.S.-PRC relations.

Since 1982, congressional interest in a larger decision-making role has declined to an extremely low level. It is now established custom that, on major arms sales to the ROC, administration officials at the office level inform the staff—not the members—of the committees of jurisdiction when decisions have already been made. Individual members may express themselves on specific transfers, and they are consulted on a case-by-case basis. But that is the limited extent to which Congress now seeks to affect the formulation of decisions.

Why has the Congress accepted administration dominance of ROC arms sale decisions? Three factors are at work. First, most of the leaders of the House Foreign Affairs Committee and the Senate Foreign Relations Committee, such as Senators Church, Javits, Percy, and Glenn and Congressmen Wolff and Solarz, were committed to developing U.S.-PRC relations and not to undermining administration policy. They saw arms sales to the ROC as an issue to be managed rather than as an invitation to interbranch struggle.

As the TRA was being drafted, these leaders sought to use the Act's language to assuage the concerns of those most concerned about the ROC's security. Yet they did not act on the procedural implications of the policy enacted; all they asked of the executive branch was to be informed in a timely way of major changes in policy.[54] Indeed, the June 1980 exchange between Wolff and Holbrooke cited above can be read as a reminder by the former to the latter that their joint interest in keeping the friends of Taiwan quiet would not be served if Wolff first learned about controversial Taiwan initiatives in the *New York Times*.

By and large, this conflict-management approach was repeated with respect to the August 1982 communiqué. Those who complained loudest were conservative Republicans who had expected something

different from their president. The congressional foreign policy mainstream, made up of centrist Republicans and Democrats, allowed their
colleagues on the right to express their frustration. But in the main
they worked to preserve rather than undermine what they saw as an
important foreign policy relationship.

The second reason why the congressional role in the decision-
making process has been a relatively minor issue is that, since the August 1982 communiqué, the Reagan administration has shaped the
content of policy in ways that have been satisfactory to the Congress.
Conservatives remained frustrated over the failure to provide an advanced fighter. Yet, because most in Congress were not concerned
over substance—probably because the government on Taiwan has
been moderately satisfied with U.S. arms transfers since 1983—members saw no need to do battle over process.

The third reason for Congress's failure to assert itself on arms sale
decisions is the institution's short attention span. Members and staff
who had taken the lead in responding to the normalization package
and who took pride in drafting the TRA either moved on to other,
more pressing issues or moved out of the institution altogether. Taking their place were individuals with other priorities. Consequently,
even the level of consultation faded as a matter of concern. It does not
require too much cynicism, moreover, to assume that the executive
branch relies on Congress's inability to follow up on those issues
where it has momentarily asserted itself. From an institutional perspective, the aftermath of the TRA reflects a general pattern in which
the executive branch rides out the firestorm of the moment and later
resumes its exclusive control over arms sale issues. A smart administration will co-opt the relevant members of Congress by keeping
them informed of decisions, but it will make the decisions all
the same.[55]

Implementation of
Arms Sale Policy

Unencumbered by any direction or pressure from
Congress, the executive branch has been free to interpret the phrase
"sufficient self-defense capability" as it wishes. Although the arms sale
decision-making process is closed to outside scrutiny, the actions and
public statements of the Carter and Reagan administrations provide a
good sense of the criteria employed.

The calculus begins with an assessment of PRC capabilities and intentions. Testifying before the Senate Foreign Relations Committee in August 1982, Assistant Secretary of State John Holdridge outlined the process:

> Let me say first of all, we will be watching the situation carefully through the various means available to us. And when I say watching the situation, I mean in the military sense in terms of deployment and capabilities; I mean in the political sense in terms of policies which are being implemented, taken in conjunction with the situation along the Taiwan Strait on both sides, the military capability for Taiwan—all of these things go into the equation.[56]

In terms of military capabilities, the U.S. government has concluded that the PRC can defeat Taiwan. At the same hearing, Holdridge said, "The way things stand today, if the People's Republic of China wanted to take Taiwan by force of arms, it could do so, even with the military situation as it now exists, in which there are certain technological advantages Taiwan possesses. Regardless, if China wanted to throw in the masses of men and matériel and the effort into taking Taiwan, Taiwan could be taken."[57]

Qualifying that judgment is a belief that the PRC would have a difficult time getting its ground forces across the Taiwan Strait to follow up an air and naval assault. The letter that the Subcommittee on Asian and Pacific Affairs sent to President Reagan in June 1981 reported that the experts it had consulted agreed that, "given the amphibious deficiencies of the Chinese armed forces, there would be ample warning time in the event the PRC commenced an effort to provide itself with the kind of sea-lift capacity they [sic] would need to effectively invade and invest Taiwan."[58]

The executive branch takes several factors into account in assessing PRC intentions. The first is Beijing's stated intention, which provides a mixed picture. On the positive side is the official commitment, as stated in the August 1982 communiqué, to a "fundamental policy to strive for a peaceful solution to the Taiwan question." Teng Hsiao-p'ing reiterated a variation of this formulation in a 1984 speech: "We stand for the peaceful reunification with Taiwan, which is part of our sacred territory."[59]

On the negative side, Beijing has never forsworn the use of force vis-à-vis Taiwan because, its officials say, the conflict is an internal one, and the absence of a military threat would leave the Nationalists with no incentive to negotiate. And, from time to time, Chinese leaders have indicated circumstances under which their peaceful intentions could change. In January 1979, Teng told a group of senators that China would be obliged to use force if Taiwan moved toward the Soviet Union for help or if Taipei indefinitely refused to enter into negotiations with Beijing.[60]

In a May 1985 interview, Hu Yao-pang, then party general secretary, acknowledged that China did not have the strength to deal with Taiwan militarily but that it might by the 1992–1995 period. At that point, "if the broad masses of the Taiwan people wish to return and only a few say no, we will have to use some force on them." Stating the point somewhat differently, Hu said in the same conversation that "if [in 1995] we have the strength to enforce a blockade and if Taiwan vehemently opposes reunification, we shall have to consider enforcing a blockade."[61] Hu's statement was not repeated in the official media, and it may not have been authoritative.

In August 1987, a Beijing radio broadcast beamed to Taiwan suggested a change in what might spur a PRC attack. It cited with approval a statement by Teng Hsiao-p'ing that "no one knows when Taiwan will be taken away again." The broadcast then asserted that "the proliferation of the view of self-determination for Taiwan is the result of provocation and instigation by anti-China forces in the international community, whose goal is to separate Taiwan from China forever." And it drew this conclusion: "When foreigners are playing tricks in an attempt to snatch Taiwan away, the Chinese government will be compelled to use force to defend national sovereignty."[62]

The second factor used to evaluate PRC intentions is the deployment of forces of the People's Liberation Army (PLA). John Holdridge said in August 1982, "I can conceive of a situation where there might be a threat along the Sino-Soviet border, for example, where China would want to increase its military strength considerably . . . If those [forces] appeared to be pointed in the direction of the Soviet Union and not Taiwan, I do not think our basic judgment would necessarily change." Increased deployments on the relatively deserted Taiwan front would call into question its peaceful policy.[63]

A third factor used to gauge PRC intentions is the putative risks it would run by attacking Taiwan. Among these are the losses that Nationalist defenses would inflict on any PLA offensive. Even Martin Lasater, who is not inclined to accept U.S. government estimates at face value, has concluded that a PRC invasion would be extremely costly:

> It is possible that Taiwan's fighters can be swept out of the sky, but only if the PRC loses a minimum of 400–500 planes. The ROC Navy can eventually be sunk, but only at the cost of several submarines, many surface craft, and many airplanes. And with enough effort, a million or so PLA soldiers could be landed on Taiwan, but only at a horrendous cost in PRC manpower and military equipment.[64]

China's leaders appear to share this assessment and its implications. In October 1984, Teng reportedly told a group of Japanese visitors that "now China does not have the military force to invade and occupy Taiwan." He did say that the capabilities existed to blockade the Taiwan Strait. In May 1985, Hu Yao-pang indicated that Beijing would use force against Taiwan "only when we are sure of complete victory," a criterion consistent with PLA doctrine.[65]

A second type of risk concerns the political losses the PRC would presumably incur through military action: a severe setback to the civilian modernization program, for which a peaceful international environment is essential; a serious deterioration in relations with Japan and the United States, on which the PRC depends primarily for technology and markets; a total negation of the recent progress Beijing has made in stimulating contacts with the ROC.

This evaluation of PRC capabilities and intentions by the executive branch results in a relatively low threat assessment. It is a view apparently shared by the Nationalist military, as reflected in a May 1988 newspaper interview given by General Hau Pei-ts'un, chief of the general staff:

> Conceding that the nation's fighting force is greatly outnumbered by the 3.5 million PLA, Hau said that the ROC enjoys an edge in terms of quality. "Although they are numerically stronger, . . . the space for military maneuvers in Taiwan is limited. Because of the space restriction, they cannot throw all their jet fighters and ground troops into the battlefield . . . " Hau said Peking would have to dispatch its fighter planes and ground troops by batches to invade . . . The ROC, with its 30 divisions, would be able to meet each successive wave of invaders with numerical superiority, . . . [and] the same would be true for air battles . . . Hau said he believes that of the various war options open to Peking, a blockade of the Taiwan Strait is most likely. He said that the ROC armed forces are still prepared

for that eventuality. The ROC would deal the enemy such a counter-blow that it would be unable to withstand it.[66]

So relaxed is the U.S. executive branch about the low level of threat to the ROC's security that it has been willing, in the interests of good relations with Beijing, to place limitations on the way it implements arms sale policy.

The first limitation, which was accepted at the time of normalization, is to supply only "defensive" weapons. What makes a weapon system defensive may be debated endlessly, but it is clear from past practice that, in the case of Taiwan, the United States means weapons for tactical defense. In his September 1978 meeting with Ch'ai Tze-min, Jimmy Carter referred to "carefully selected arms sales . . . that would not be threatening to China."[67] Among the criteria his administration used in deciding what arms to sell to Taiwan were range and offensive capability against the PRC.[68] Alexander Haig reported that the Pentagon thought that Taiwan's defense needs "could be met by an interceptor with limited avionics that would present no threat to China."[69]

As noted previously, there lurks a latent contradiction between the commitment the administration made to Beijing concerning defensive arms, as that term appears to be understood, and the objective of the TRA for a sufficient self-defense capability for Taiwan. Tactically offensive weapons may be used in the service of strategic defense. Were China ever to mount an attack on Taiwan or even prepare to do so, it would be in Taiwan's interest to take out mainland airfields and naval staging areas. Having the capacity to do so would enhance the deterrent capabilities of Taiwan's armed forces.

The second self-imposed limitation, made through the August 1982 communiqué, was to cap and then reduce the dollar value of arms sold to Taiwan. The stated rationale for this restraint—that "if China continues to maintain a peaceful approach to the Taiwan question, then [Taiwan's] needs will be reduced commensurately."[70]—is totally fallacious. It might be true if PRC capabilities did not improve, which of course they will. And it would only be true if Taiwan's planes and ships never wore out, which of course they will.

Yet the Reagan administration mitigated the effect of this limitation by interpreting it flexibly. When it came time to set the dollar amount of arms sales in fiscal year 1983, it took the dollar amount for the highest year since normalization ($587 million in FY 1979), expressed that amount in 1983 dollars ($830 million), and then set a FY 1983 target of $800 million. Since that time, the administration has

Value of U.S. Arms Sales to Taiwan
($ million)

Fiscal Year	Foreign Military Sales Agreements	Commercial Exports	Total
1983	698.6	85.0	783.6
1984	688.7	70.0	758.7
1985	700.4	54.5	754.9
1986	510.8	228.4	739.2
1987	509.6	210.0	719.6

SOURCE: U.S. Department of Defense, Defense Security Assistance Agency, *Foreign Military Sales, Foreign Military Construction Sales and Military Assistance Facts* (September 30, 1987). Foreign military sales concern items sold from U.S. government arsenals. Commercial exports are items sold by the manufacturer after a license has been secured from the State Department's Office of Munitions Control. Because it is impossible to time arms sale transactions to the fiscal year, the actual declines do not always equal $20 million per year.

projected a $20 million decline in foreign military sales agreements and commercial-license sales combined. The actual amounts are shown in the table.

The third limitation, also accepted through the August 1982 communiqué, is to refrain from providing the ROC with military equipment that exceeds the quality of that provided in the early normalization years. Again, it is somewhat spurious to justify holding quality constant solely because the PRC states peaceful intentions. The ROC's arsenal was not exactly state of the art at the time the communiqué was signed, and PRC capabilities are certain to improve with time. It is also difficult to maintain a constant quality level when weapons systems are always changing.

For this latter reason, the Reagan administration has taken the liberty of interpreting this element of the communiqué in a flexible way. A good example was the sale of twelve C-130s in June 1984. These planes were replacements for C-119 transports that could no longer be flown safely. The C-130 was definitely a qualitative improvement over what Taiwan had, and between 1979 and 1982 the ROC had received no transport planes. Because the U.S. government no longer had anything of a lower quality than the C-130, these were all that it could provide.[71]

Beijing has objected to Washington's flexible interpretation of the quality and quantity limitations, charging that specific transfers violate the August 1982 communiqué.[72] These criticisms, however, have not been vociferous, and the PRC has not seen fit to reopen the issue. It should not be assumed that these responses are purely ritualistic and will not be repeated. During President Reagan's visit to China in April 1984, Foreign Minister Hsueh-ch'ien asked Secretary of State George Shultz to reduce the dollar value of arms transfers to Taiwan by $100 million per year, five times faster than the current rate.[73]

What does the concept of "sufficient self-defense capability" mean as far as the U.S. executive branch is concerned? Based on its behavior for almost a decade, the United States does not define the ROC's defense needs to mean the ability to mount a full-scale defense against a full-scale PRC attack. An invasion or blockade is deemed to be an "imaginary horrible" whose probability is so low that it is effectively disregarded.

Washington appears to believe that the ROC should have the ability to inflict a significant cost on attacking mainland forces should deterrence fail, if only to prevent Beijing from considering intimidation and blackmail. To that end, the United States has focused its arms sales on air and naval defense and has provided fighter interceptors, surface-to-air missiles, and antisubmarine warfare equipment.

In retrospect, however, Washington was not satisfied with assuring modest yet significant deterrence for the ROC while living within the pledges made to Beijing. Rather than trying to square the circle, U.S. and KMT officials decided to create a new geometry for the arms sale issue.

From Imports to Import Substitution

After the August 1982 communiqué, the government on Taiwan determined that it could no longer depend on the United States to sell it advanced weapons systems "off the shelf" and that it would have to develop the capacity to manufacture those weapons itself.

It is not known precisely when and how it was decided to take this step. There are hints that greater self-reliance was more popular within the Nationalist high command than in the Foreign Ministry, which may have placed greater value on the political benefits that flowed from the ROC's dependence on the United States.[74] If such a schism existed, Chiang Ching-kuo sided with his generals. Also unclear is the extent to which the United States encouraged this transition. One may surmise, however, that President Reagan was far more likely to pledge U.S. cooperation with indigenous weapons development in Taiwan than his predecessor.

The ROC's program to manufacture weapons for defense has already been described in recent publications.[75] That program's underlying objective was to achieve three goals: control of the territorial air space and approach routes, control of the Taiwan Strait plus its sea lanes in case of blockade, and repulsing any amphibious assaults. Wherever possible, old weapons systems were to be modernized to extend their life span and increase their firepower. But the heart of the program was to develop new systems—a fleet of frigates with antiship, antisubmarine, and antiaircraft capabilities; advanced fighter aircraft; modernized main battle tanks; and a range of ground-to-air, air-to-air, and antiship missiles.

All these new systems were designed to replace obsolete items in the ROC's inventory that will be retired sooner or later—frigates for aging destroyers, fighters for American F-104 and F5E interceptors, and new missiles for Hawks, Nikes, and Sidewinders. In addition, the ROC can produce the weapons it has been unable to purchase from the United States—an advanced fighter instead of the FX, and the Hsiung Feng-2 antiship missile instead of the Harpoon.

United States firms now provide technological assistance, including design and construction, once their transfers have been approved by a government review board composed of representatives of the departments of State and Defense. If the items to be transferred to the ROC are on the munitions control or commodity control lists, U.S. firms must first secure export licenses from the U.S. government. All major production facilities are located in the ROC. In the frigate program, for example, Todd Pacific Shipyard of Seattle and the Bath Iron Works in Maine competed to transfer the technology, and the ROC's China Shipbuilding Corporation constructs the hulls. A key institution in the ROC for the development of many of the systems is the Chung Shan Institute of Science and Technology in Taoyuan, the government's key defense-related research and development facility.

Obviously, the move to import substitution for advanced weapons systems has transformed the whole arms sale issue. As long as the United States is willing to continue a program of technology transfer, as long as the government on Taiwan is able to commit some of its human and budgetary resources to the costly effort to build a military-industrial complex, and as long as the PRC places a relatively low priority on defense modernization, the ROC can gradually enhance its capacity to deter a PRC attack. The ROC will also gain the confidence that comes from having made that accomplishment.

Beijing's response to this new development has been restrained. The only public commentaries from the PRC came when the issue was raised by the U.S. foreign policy specialist Selig Harrison. He asked Hu Yao-pang about technology transfer during an April 1986 interview. Hu reportedly challenged the Reagan administration claim that technology transfer was permitted under the August 1982 communiqué. "Arms sales and the transfer of technology for arms manufacture are the same thing," Hu said.[76] Then, in July 1986, the overseas edition of the Chinese journal *Liaowang* featured an extensive discussion of a *Los Angeles Times* article by Harrison that reviewed his conversation with Hu. The author of the *Liaowang* article equated the transfer of weapons technology to the ROC with "openly infringing upon sovereignty and directly interfering in China's internal affairs" in a way that "has not only seriously violated the principles of the '17 August Communiqué,' but also departed from international practice."[77]

Around the same time, Beijing reportedly queried Washington privately as to whether technology transfer did not violate the spirit of the 1982 communiqué. In mid August, the Reagan administration replied that it would take the document into account in its dealings with the ROC and that the communiqué did not need reinterpretation or renegotiation. An unidentified U.S. official was more specific in an interview with the *Far Eastern Economic Review:* "The text is very clear. It talks of arms sales and not technology."[78]

Arming Both Sides of the Strait

It is perhaps a measure of the Reagan administration's confidence in its ability to manage the issue of arms sales to the ROC that it not only accepted the limitations of the August 1982 communiqué but also undertook to sell arms to the PRC. The latter initiative could have been politically explosive if not properly handled. A. Doak Barnett described the problem as follows:

> If U.S.-China military cooperation and arms sales grow, so too in all probability will pressures (both from Taipei and from the U.S. Congress) to increase the level and sophistication of weapons sales to Taiwan. But if Washington were to sell larger quantities or more advanced versions of military equipment to Taipei, this probably would trigger another political crisis in U.S.-China relations, which could abort any attempts to expand cooperative military ties between Washington and Beijing.[79]

The administration avoided being caught in a crossfire in two ways: It kept key congressional actors informed and anticipated their concerns, and it changed the terms of the debate in ways that Barnett—and many conservatives—could not have predicted.

Arms sales to the PRC became a real possibility after the mid 1983 upswing in U.S.-PRC relations and Secretary Caspar Weinberger's September 1983 visit to Beijing.[80] On a regular basis thereafter, administration officials briefed key staff of the House Foreign Affairs Committee and, presumably, the Senate Foreign Relations Committee as well. Consequently, those members who would have to manage the congressional reaction once sales were announced had the opportunity to tell administration officials that military transfer to the PRC would only be a serious problem if the PRC began to threaten the ROC militarily.

Prior to the administration's formal notification of Congress, the House Foreign Affairs Committee had arranged briefings for Committee staff and the foreign affairs staffs of Committee members, especially of those members most likely to worry about sales to the PRC. If those members could be convinced at the outset that providing a particular weapons system to the PRC definitely had an anti–Soviet or anti–Vietnamese purpose and that the ROC's security would not be further endangered, problems were less likely to arise. But if the ROC government decided that a particular U.S. weapon sale to the PRC risked the ROC's security, and if the ROC communicated that view to its friends in Congress, the administration might not be able to persuade conservative members to support its policy.

Since the fall of 1985, when the Reagan administration began reaching arms sale agreements with the PRC, only the sale of avionics kits to enhance the F-8 aircraft aroused congressional concern. News of that sale surfaced in late December 1985 and early January 1986, and advance consultation was not enough to defuse conservative members' concerns.

The principal catalyst for opposition to the sale of avionics kits was the Heritage Foundation, whose director for Asian studies, Martin Lasater, had frequently written about the U.S.-PRC security relationship. As soon as news of the avionics sale became known, Lasater circulated position papers arguing that providing the avionics for the F-8 would give the PRC air force an all-weather capability that the ROC did not have, and that would tip the military balance in the PRC's favor. In the event that the sale to the PRC went ahead, he said, the TRA required that the United States provide either the F-20 Tigershark or the F-16 to the ROC.[81]

Lasater also searched for congressional advocates of his position.

In early February, Congressman Philip Crane circulated for signature a letter to the president asking him to reconsider the sale. On March 15, Senator Barry Goldwater took the floor of the Senate to criticize the "flawed mentality" of selling arms to the PRC.[82] Lasater's main supporters were Jesse Helms in the Senate and Mark Siljander, a junior representative from Michigan, in the House. They introduced resolutions of disapproval after the administration notified Congress on April 8 that it was taking action. Siljander also introduced a resolution that would have allowed the sale only if the U.S. sold advanced fighters to the ROC.

The committees of jurisdiction and the administration then went into action. In the House, the Subcommittee on Asian and Pacific Affairs held a classified briefing on April 17 so that members could hear the intelligence community's analysis of how the avionics package would benefit PRC security and whether it would result in an increased threat to the ROC. The Senate Foreign Relations Committee held a public hearing on April 29. Simultaneously, executive branch representatives met individually with members who were or might be opposed to sale and brought them up to date on the full scope of U.S. security cooperation with the ROC.

Then, on May 1, the Senate Foreign Relations Committee voted 14–1 to reject the resolution of disapproval. Senator Jesse Helms was the only vote in favor, an indication that the administration's lobbying effort among other Republicans had been successful.[83] The members most concerned about ROC security had had second thoughts about pushing their effort any further; securing resounding endorsements for arms sales to the PRC had not really been their objective.

In the House, Congressman Siljander made the best of a bad situation. At a May 7 hearing of the Asian Affairs Subcommittee, he announced that, based on a meeting that he and three colleagues had had on April 29 with State and Defense Department officials, and in return for administration "assurances that our relationship with Taiwan regarding defense as outlined in the Taiwan Relations Act will be met, and will be met in full," he was withdrawing his resolutions.[84] In fact, those assurances were nothing more than an argument that the ROC's security could be preserved by technology transfer instead of the sale of advanced fighter aircraft.

Realistically, there was little chance that Congress could have stopped the avionics sale if the administration had insisted on going forward because a two-thirds majority would have been necessary to override a presidential veto of a resolution of disapproval. But had the opponents of the sale been able to stimulate extensive public discussion about linking arms sales to both the PRC and the ROC, the PRC might have decided that a military relationship with the United States was not in its interest. Yet the opponents—all conservative Republicans—could never convince any of their colleagues that a serious problem existed. That they failed to do so reflects how Congress has accepted the U.S. relationship with the PRC and the ability of the Reagan administration to demonstrate its commitment to preserve the ROC's security. Much has changed since the TRA became law.

Conclusion

It is easy to exaggerate the arms sale provision of the TRA as law. It is part of a law, and it is cast in legal form. Yet, as this discussion has revealed, the provision did not actually mandate a change either in the behavior of the administration or in the institutional relations between the legislative and executive branches. In particular, the Congress never saw fit to define the key term *sufficient self-defense capability*. As a result, the president received broad discretion to implement the arms sale provision of the TRA as he saw fit.

Different administrations have interpreted the provision in different ways at different times. Although the Carter administration took a relaxed view of the threat facing the ROC, it did, under pressure from Congress, authorize U.S. fighter aircraft manufacturers to begin discussions with the Nationalists on the FX. Whether a second Carter administration would have been willing and able to provide an advanced fighter can only be a matter of speculation.

Early in the first Reagan administration, some officials advocated selling the FX, but ultimately the Carter administration's threat assessment prevailed, and the idea was dropped. In addition, the limitations of the August 1982 communiqué were accepted. Faced with the looming obsolescence of the ROC's military equipment, however, President Reagan was willing to help the island's armed forces preserve a basic deterrent by facilitating the transfer of weapons technology.

How has the ROC's security fared under the TRA? Will the gradual modernization of the People's Liberation Army progressively tilt the balance in the PRC's favor? The most sophisticated assessments of these questions, done by the intelligence agencies of the relevant governments, are not available for public review. The most remarkable development in recent years, however, has been the confidence that the Nationalist military has exhibited regarding its ability to defend the island—even though Taipei would have an understandable incentive to minimize its prowess and play up the threat posed by its adversaries. The clearest expression of this optimism is the statement of General Hao Pei-ts'un cited previously. In the minds of those whose opinions count the most, therefore, implementation of the TRA has not jeopardized Taiwan's security.

Yet, another administration might choose to implement the TRA in ways that were consistent with the law yet far less favorable to the ROC than President Reagan's approach. Policy makers could accept Beijing's definition of the situation, that ROC arms sales are an obstacle to both good U.S.-PRC relations and the reunification of China. Based on that assumption, the military threat to Taiwan could be defined as being so small that only a limited security relationship with the island would be justified. Washington might add insult to Taipei's injury by acceding to Beijing's desire that the United States encourage the Nationalists to negotiate with their communist adversaries. The words of the TRA would not bar such a course.

The arms sale provision of the TRA is, therefore, less important as law than as an expression of a fundamental political commitment. It serves as an indicator of a consensus within the U.S. body politic, and particularly within the Congress, that Taiwan should not be taken over by force, that it should not be intimidated into submission, and that it should not settle with the mainland until it is absolutely ready.

This consensus is broad. It runs from conservatives on the right who do not wish to see the United States betray its friends in the Kuomintang once more to liberals on the left who identify with the democratic aspirations of the Taiwanese people. The consensus is basically passive and can be mobilized only when Taiwan is manifestly in danger. The ROC can activate the consensus if it decides to draw on all the good will that has been built up in the Congress and in the public over the years. As such, this consensus constitutes a real deterrent to an administration that would yield too quickly, should Beijing decide to reopen the Taiwan issue.

This political commitment is not new, of course. It has been an important factor in the long and complex struggle between the KMT and the Communist Party. The situation became more complex once the leaders in Beijing became able to counter Taiwan's advantage by appealing to the U.S. executive branch. The two sides of the Chinese civil war have thus threatened to play the two branches of the U.S. government against each other.

Since 1983, this quadrilateral relationship has stabilized. The Reagan administration by and large acted in accordance with the congressionally based commitment to the ROC, and Congress did not object to its initiatives toward Beijing. As a result, there has recently been more consensus on PRC and ROC policy between the executive branch and Congress and within the Congress than at any time since World War II. For their parts, both Beijing and Taipei are moderately satisfied with their U.S. relationships. Neither has felt the need or had the ability to encircle the other by marching through Washington. And the two sides are now beginning to deal tentatively but directly with each other.

Both U.S. politics and international politics should incline the Bush administration to continue the policies of its predecessor. The only question is whether Beijing will choose to reopen the issue of the U.S.-ROC security relationship. Although it is, of course, too early even to guess at an answer, Beijing's likely agenda of protest is easily imagined. The basis for protest would be Washington's interpretation of the August 1982 communiqué, including the following points:

- its use of an inflation factor for setting the ceiling on the quantity of arms sales to Taiwan;
- its low $20 million per year reductions in arms sales to Taipei since 1983;
- its flexible interpretation of the restrictions on the quality of arms sold to Taipei;
- its unwillingness, despite PRC entreaties, to press Taipei to negotiate on "peaceful reunification," progress which might dictate faster reductions in arms sales to Taipei;
- most of all, its view that the transfer of defense technology is outside the scope of the August 1982 communiqué.

There are those who suggest that the United States should base its policy on the assumption that the PRC will reopen the arms transfer issue. Selig Harrison, for one, believes that Beijing will eventually react to these various examples of an "American posture toward the future of Taiwan [that] is not genuinely detached." In his view, the arms sale issue "has become a rasping psychological irritant to the entire American relationship with Beijing." To the PRC, "it symbolizes American bad faith, coupled with a patronizing posture in which the United States assumes that it holds all the cards and takes China's friendship for granted."[85] Implicitly, Harrison advocates that Washington end the program of defense technology transfer and respond to reduced tensions in the Taiwan Strait by accelerating the reduction of weapons transfers.[86] Without such efforts to defuse the arms sale issue, xenophobic dissatisfaction with Washington's Taiwan policy could, after Teng Hsiao-p'ing's death, "become a weapon in the hands of domestic critics of close economic, military and intelligence-sharing ties with the United States."[87]

Yet, because we cannot know whether the PRC will, in fact, reopen the Taiwan issue, the United States government need not act as if a crisis is imminent. If President Bush announces that the United States will shape its policy according to the principles set forth in the relevant communiqués (as the U.S. government has understood them), if he neither acts like he wants a "two-China" outcome nor talks openly about the transfer of defense technology to Taiwan, and if he seeks to ensure that the economic heart of the relationship is sound as the end of the Teng era nears, there is every reason to believe that Beijing will downplay the arms sale issue.

Indeed, Beijing forced the 1981 downturn in relations for a variety of reasons, not simply because of ROC arms sales, and its hostility did not end once the August 1982 communiqué was issued, but only after Washington initiated a significant liberalization of its policy of technology transfer to the PRC in May 1983. If the PRC formally objects to the continuing U.S. security relationship with the ROC, it will probably also have complaints about its insufficient access to export markets and high technology and about the U.S. role in the world.

If the PRC were to complain, it is not clear that the United States would necessarily listen. The PRC's perceived strategic value to the United States has declined since normalization. Both Beijing and Washington's relations with Moscow have changed, and in recent years Beijing has not consistently worked in parallel with the United States in regional conflicts in which both are involved. Indeed, the arms sale relationship that currently undermines U.S.-PRC relations is not Washington's relations with Taipei but Beijing's relations with the countries of the Persian Gulf and the Middle East. China's missile transfers to Iran, Saudi Arabia, and Syria have threatened either U.S. lives (sailors in the Persian Gulf) or U.S. vital interests (the security of Israel), created foreign policy problems for the U.S. government, and unsettled U.S. public opinion.

Even Beijing's specific complaints on the arms sale issue would not necessarily be justified. With respect to the August 1982 communiqué itself, the United States should not be held solely responsible for the document's ambiguities and loopholes. Since the terms *quality* and *quantity* were not defined, U.S. officials had leave to interpret them.

On the central point, moreover, the communiqué plainly refers only to arms [*wu-ch'i*] and not to arms technology [*wu-ch'i chi-shu*]. Moreover, the PRC should take some responsibility for its statements about the circumstances under which it would use force, for they could call into question the PRC's pledge in the communiqué to strive for a peaceful resolution of the issue of reunification with Taiwan.

It should be emphasized, moreover, that the PRC's rationale for demanding reduced arms sales has been shown to be fallacious. Beijing claimed that Taipei would be less likely to negotiate and permit contacts if the United States provided it with the means to defend itself. Yet recent experience has shown that the government on Taiwan became responsive to PRC overtures when it became more secure militarily. Given the political influence of Taiwan's military and the salience of national security on the island, it is unlikely that President Chiang Ching-kuo would have taken his mainland initiatives if his armed forces had lacked confidence in their improving deterrent capability. There are other reasons, to be sure, of Taipei's new openness, but this one is certainly significant.

If the leaders in Beijing and Taipei are ever to resolve their differences, they should do so through mutual engagement and not through the United States. The fundamental source of their conflict is an absence of trust, which can only be created by the direct contact that has recently begun.

However that process of mutual engagement plays out, the United States should not become a party to it. But it can continue to create a context. In that regard, the members of Congress who wrote the TRA made their contribution. More by luck than by design, perhaps, they succeeded in providing a measure of security for the government and people on Taiwan through the expression of a political commitment that the Reagan administration was later prepared to act upon. As a result, the ROC has become confident that it can deter the PLA over the long term militarily and so engage Beijing on an equal basis politically. This was probably not the outcome intended by the TRA's authors, but it is one from which they might take some satisfaction.

Appendix A

Extract from the August 1982 Communiqué

. . .

2. The question of United States arms sales to Taiwan was not settled in

the course of negotiations between the two countries on establishing diplomatic relations. The two sides held differing positions, and the Chinese side stated that it would raise the issue again following normalization. Recognizing that this issue would seriously hamper the development of United States-China relations, they have held further discussions of it . . .

3. Respect for each other's sovereignty and territorial integrity and non-interference in each other's internal affairs constitute the fundamental principles guiding United States-China relations. These principles were confirmed in the Shanghai Communiqué on the Establishment of Diplomatic Relations which came into effect on January 1, 1979. Both sides emphatically state that these principles continue to govern all aspects of their relations.

4. The Chinese government reiterates that the question of Taiwan is China's internal affair. The Message to Compatriots in Taiwan issued by China on January 1, 1979 promulgated a fundamental policy of striving for peaceful reunification of the Motherland. The Nine-Point Proposal put forward by China on September 30, 1981 represented a further major effort under this fundamental policy to strive for a peaceful solution to the Taiwan question.

5. The United States Government attaches great importance to its relations with China, and reiterates that it has no intention of infringing on Chinese sovereignty and territorial integrity, or interfering in China's internal affairs, or pursuing a policy of "two Chinas" or "one China, one Taiwan." The United States Government understands and appreciates the Chinese policy of striving for a peaceful resolution of the Taiwan question as indicated in China's Message to Compatriots in Taiwan issued on January 1, 1979 and the Nine-Point Proposal put forward by China on September 30, 1981. The new situation which has emerged with regard to the Taiwan question also provides favorable conditions for the settlement of United States-China differences over the question of United States arms sales to Taiwan.

6. Having in mind the foregoing statements of both sides, the United States Government states that it does not seek to carry out a long-term policy of arms sales to Taiwan, that its arms sales to Taiwan will not exceed, either in qualitative or quantitative terms, the level of those supplied in recent years since the establishment of diplomatic relations between the United States and China, and that it intends to reduce gradually its sales of arms to Taiwan, leading over a period of time to a final resolution. In so stating, the United States acknowledges China's consistent position regarding the thorough settlement of this issue.

Notes

1. For an examination of the TRA as a case study of post-Vietnam legislative activism, see Cecil V. Crabb, Jr., "An Assertive Congress and the TRA: Policy Influences and Implications," in Louis W. Koenig, James C. Hsiung, and King-yuh Chang (eds.), *Congress, the Presidency, and the Taiwan Relations Act* (New York: Praeger, 1985), pp. 85–110.

2. See U.S. Congress, House of Representatives, Committee on Foreign Affairs, "Executive-Legislative Consultations on China Policy, 1978–79," Congress and Foreign Policy Series, no. 1 (Washington, D.C.: Government Printing Office, 1980); Cyrus Vance, *Hard Choices* (New York: Simon & Schuster, 1983), p. 118. Before the announcement of the normalization agreement, Vance argued strenuously for informing the Congress but was overruled.

3. The four works are Zbigniew Brzezinski, *Power and Principle: Memoirs of the National Security Adviser, 1977–1981* (New York: Farrar, Straus & Giroux, 1983); Jimmy Carter, *Keeping Faith: Memoirs of a President* (New York: Bantam, 1982); Michel Oksenberg, "A Decade of Sino-American Relations," *Foreign Affairs* 61, no. 1 (Fall 1982): 181–88; Cyrus Vance, *Hard Choices*.

4. *Wall Street Journal,* October 4, 1977.

5. Oksenberg, "Sino-American Relations," p. 182.

6. Vance, *Hard Choices,* p. 82; Brzezinski, *Power and Principle,* p. 208.

7. Vance, *Hard Choices,* pp. 115–16.

8. Brzezinski, *Power and Principle,* p. 229.

9. Vance carried with him the draft of a normalization communiqué, but even before he reached Beijing he was inclined not to table it. The Panama Canal treaties were making their way through a hostile Congress; to have broken relations with Taiwan at that point would have, in his view, overloaded the Washington political circuits (Vance, *Hard Choices,* pp. 79 and following.) Brzezinski told Carter on his return that arms sales were not raised "directly." The subject was discussed: Hua Kuo-feng asserted that "for the United States to sell arms and request China to commit itself to a peaceful resolution of the issue would clearly lead to a 'two-China solution.'" What is significant is that Taiwan arms sales were not brought up as a U.S. condition for normalization (Brzezinski, *Power and Principle,* pp. 218–19).

10. The U.S. timing is clear from Oksenberg's account ("Sino-American Relations," pp. 187–88). It was only after Woodcock's December 4 meeting with Huang Hua, his last with the foreign minister, that Washington decided that the Chinese "seemed prepared to absorb the arms sales issue and negotiate on a recognition communiqué." The report of Chinese reticence is based on a personal communication from a knowledgeable U.S. official.

11. Brzezinski, *Power and Principle,* p. 214. (Emphasis added.)

12. This may be inferred from Vance, *Hard Choices,* p. 115.

13. Oksenberg, "Sino-American Relations," p. 187.

14. Brzezinski, *Power and Principle,* p. 231.

15. Oksenberg, "Sino-American Relations," p. 188.

16. Brzezinski, *Power and Principle,* p. 231.

17. Oksenberg, "Sino-American Relations," p. 188. Hua Kuo-feng stated the Chinese view at the time of normalization. At a Beijing press conference on December 16, he said: "During the negotiations the U.S. side mentioned

that after normalization it would continue to sell limited amounts of arms to Taiwan for defensive purposes. We made it clear that we absolutely would not agree to this. In all discussions the Chinese side repeatedly made clear its position on this question. We held that after the normalization continued sales of arms to Taiwan by the United States would not conform to the principles of the normalization, would be detrimental to the peaceful liberation of Taiwan and would exercise an unfavourable influence on the peace and stability of the Asia-Pacific region. So our two sides had differences on this point. Nevertheless, we reached an agreement on the joint communiqué." Lester L. Wolff and David L. Simon, eds., *Legislative History of the Taiwan Relations Act: An Analytical Compilation with Documents on Subsequent Developments* (Jamaica, N.Y.: American Association for Chinese Studies, 1982), p. 304.

18. All citations to the TRA are to Public Law 96–8, April 10, 1979 (Washington, D.C.: Government Printing Office).

19. In light of the history of U.S. security policy in Asia, the TRA provisions implementing the arms sale policy are consistent with the Nixon doctrine whereby the United States will provide our friends with the ability to defend themselves. Yet the authors of the TRA felt compelled to provide some vestige of the prior approach—formal security commitments enshrined in treaties. Section 3(c) of the TRA reads, "The President is directed to inform the Congress promptly of any threat to the security or the social or economic system of the people on Taiwan and any danger to the interests of the United States arising therefrom. The President and the Congress shall determine, in accordance with constitutional processes, appropriate action by the United States in response to any such danger." The good news for Taiwan in this provision is that the range of problematic PRC actions is broader than under the U.S.-ROC mutual defense treaty of 1954, which spoke only of an "armed attack." The bad news is that, under the TRA, PRC threats are deemed to be regarded only as a matter of "grave concern to the United States"; the treaty said that the United States would deem an armed attack as "dangerous to its own peace and safety." The treaty, moreover, is more definitive concerning the U.S. response: The United States "*would act* to meet the common danger in accordance with its constitutional processes" (emphasis added). Under the TRA, the Congress and the president are to determine "appropriate action." Clearly, the Vietnam War had taken its toll. For an extended discussion of the ambiguous U.S. security commitment to the ROC, see Richard M. Pious, "The Taiwan Relations Act: The Constitutional and Legal Context," in Koenig, Hsiung, and Chang (eds.), *Congress, the Presidency, and the Taiwan Relations Act*, pp. 155–64.

20. Interview with a staff member of the House Office of Legislative Counsel who was deeply involved in the drafting of the TRA.

21. Ibid.

22. Derwinski said, "This provision is meant to insure that Taiwan's defense needs are determined by its authorities and those of the United States without regard to the views of the PRC. Any attempt by the PRC to interfere

in this process would be completely contrary to the interests of the United States" (*Congressional Record*, March 28, 1979, p. H-1743). Derwinski's comments aside, the provision as enacted would permit an administration to ignore the ROC's view of its defense needs if it should choose to do.

23. Jacob K. Javits, "Congress and Foreign Relations: The Taiwan Relations Act," *Foreign Affairs*, 60, no. 1 (Fall 1981): 60.

24. U.S. Congress, House of Representatives, Committee on Foreign Affairs, *Implementation of the Taiwan Relations Act: Hearings, 96th Congress, 1st Session, October 23 and November 8, 1979* (Washington, D.C.: Government Printing Office, 1980), p. 51.

25. Interview with a staff member of the House Office of Legislative Counsel who was deeply involved in the drafting of the TRA.

26. U.S. Government Accounting Office report. The passage is quoted from an unclassified section of a document that overall is classified "secret."

27. U.S. President, *Public Papers of the Presidents of the United States. Jimmy Carter, 1979. Book I* (Washington, D.C.: Government Printing Office, 1980), pp. 640–41.

28. Personal communication.

29. There are several accounts of the 1980–1983 downturn. Among them is Robert A. Manning, "Reagan's Chance Hit," *Foreign Policy*, no. 54 (Spring 1984): 83–101. For an insider's view, see Alexander M. Haig, Jr., *Caveat: Realism, Reagan, and Foreign Policy* (New York: Macmillan, 1984).

30. Teng Hsiao-p'ing said as much to Secretary Haig during the latter's visit to Beijing. See Haig, *Caveat*, pp. 207–8. In early July, a demarche was delivered to Arthur Hummel, the U.S. ambassador in Beijing, which threatened that "if the United States continued to sell arms to Taiwan, this would force China into a very strong reaction with grave consequences for the strategic situation (ibid., p. 208).

31. Ibid., p. 210.

32. Ibid., p. 211.

33. Ibid., p. 210.

34. Ibid., p. 214.

35. Ibid., p. 213.

36. Ibid., p. 214. Note that Haig's use of the word *permitted* echoes the modulation that the Carter administration set for the TRA—that it empowered the president and did not bind him. More generally, *Washington Post* correspondent Lou Cannon developed in his reporting the theme that President Reagan would only make difficult concessions when his advisers found a way to convince him that he was maintaining, and not betraying, his fundamental principles, whatever the facts of the matter might be.

37. Wolff and Simon, pp. 321–22.

38. Ibid., p. 314.

39. Ibid., p. 319

40. The statements cited may all be found in Wolff and Simon, *Legislative History of the TRA*. The communiqué itself appears on pp. 312–13; President Reagan's statement appears on pp. 314–15; Assistant Secretary Holdridge's statement appears on pp. 316–17; and the Chinese Foreign Ministry's, on pp. 321–22.

41. U.S. Congress, House of Representatives, Committee on Foreign Affairs, *China-Taiwan: United States Policy. Hearing, August 18, 1982* (Washington, D.C.: Government Printing Office, 1982), pp. 20–21 and 24–25.

42. U.S. Congress, Senate, Committee on Foreign Relations, *U.S. Policy Toward China and Taiwan: Hearing, August 17, 1982* (Washington, D.C.: Government Printing Office, 1982), p. 3. See also the statement of Senator Helms on p. 20 and that of Representative Zablocki, chairman of the House Foreign Affairs Committee, in U.S. Congress, House of Representatives, Committee on Foreign Affairs, *China-Taiwan: United States Policy. Hearing, August 18, 1982*, pp. 1–2. In the immediate postnormalization period, the Government Accounting Office had taken only a tentative stand on the effect of PRC views on U.S. decisions. Its spokesman said, "Whether the executive branch is giving too much weight [in its ROC arms sales decisions] to the possible reaction from the PRC and the impact on future U.S.-PRC relations is a matter of judgment. The executive branch obviously has a valid concern that future sales to Taiwan not destabilize the regional military balance or be perceived as providing an offensive threat to the PRC as opposed to the maintenance of a viable Taiwan defensive capability." See U.S. Congress, Senate, Committee on Foreign Relations, Subcommittee on East Asian and Pacific Affairs, *Oversight of the Taiwan Relations Act: Hearing, May 14, 1980* (Washington, D.C.: Government Printing Office, 1980), pp. 5–6.

43. Wolff and Simon, *Legislative History of the TRA*, p. 323. This was one of the "six no's" that the Reagan administration conveyed to the Nationalists. The others were that the United States had not: (2) agreed to set a date for ending arms sales to the ROC, (3) agreed to play any mediation role between Taipei and Beijing, (4) agreed to revise the TRA, (5) altered its position regarding sovereignty over Taiwan, or (6) agreed to exert pressure on Taipei to enter into negotiations with Beijing. In congressional hearings right after the communiqué's release, members got the administration spokesman to publicly state the "six no's." See, for example, U.S. Congress, *China-Taiwan: United States Policy*, p. 22.

44. The subcommittee's proceedings are summarized in U.S. Congress, Senate, Committee on the Judiciary, Subcommittee on Separation of Powers, *Taiwan Communiqué and Separation of Powers: Report on the Taiwan Relations Act and the Joint Communiqué Signed by the United States and China* (Washington, D.C.: Government Printing Office, 1983).

45. Ibid., pp. 11, 19. Note the apparent contradiction between the higher priority that the president and administration placed on the TRA (vis-à-vis various U.S.-PRC communiqués) when it spoke to Congress and the priority Vice-President Bush placed on it during his May 1982 visit to Beijing.

46. For a discussion of the early 1983 shift in U.S. policy, see Robert Sutter's essay in this volume. The March 10, 1983 appearance of Paul Wolfowitz, who had replaced John Holdridge as assistant secretary of state for East Asian and Pacific affairs, before Senator East's subcommittee was designed to reassure conservatives about the Reagan administration's intentions. See U.S. Congress, Senate, Committee on the Judiciary, Subcommittee on Separation of Powers, *Taiwan Communiqué and Separation of Powers: Hearing. Part 2* (Washington, D.C.: Government Printing Office, 1983). (I am grateful to Robert Sutter for bringing to my attention the importance of this particular hearing.) At around the same time, the administration decided to take inflation into account in setting the ceiling from which reductions in the dollar value of U.S. arms sales to the ROC would descend.

47. U.S. Senate, *Taiwan Communiqué and Separation of Powers: Report,* p. 10.

48. Prior to June 1983, when the Supreme Court rendered a judgment in the *Chadha* case, Congress had the power to negate an arms sale decision of the executive branch by the simple-majority passage of a concurrent resolution (which is not sent to the president for signature or veto). As a result of the *Chadha* decision, Congress could only stop an arms sale by passing a law or joint resolution prohibiting it. Because both of these types of legislation are sent to the president, a two-thirds majority, sufficient to override a veto, would be necessary to ensure enactment.

49. Interview with an informed observer of U.S. government arms sale decision making.

50. U.S. Senate, *Oversight of the Taiwan Relations Act,* p. 6.

51. The Wolff-Holbrooke exchange may be found in U.S. Congress, House of Representatives, Committee on Foreign Affairs, Subcommittee on Asian and Pacific Affairs, *Implementation of the Taiwan Relations Act: Hearing, June 11, 1980* (Washington, D.C.: Government Printing Office, 1981), pp. 6–11. When asked by Chairman Wolff to distinguish consultation from notification, Holbrooke replied: "We [the executive branch] talk about a specific problem, whether it is the follow-on aircraft or customs markings or whatever. We have our responsibility to take action in that area. We come to our own conclusions as to how to proceed. We tell you what we are thinking about. If we don't hear again from you, we go ahead. If we hear from you, we are in a consultation. If we don't hear from you, we have notified you." Wolff's ire was aggravated by his belief that he had not heard about initiatives taken during Defense Secretary Brown's January 1980 trip to Beijing in a timely way.

52. U.S. Senate, *U.S. Policy Toward China and Taiwan,* pp. 1 and 5–6. See also the conclusion in U.S. Senate, *Taiwan Communiqué and the Separation of Powers,* pp. 11–12, that Senator Percy's evaluation was not a consensus view. The description of Representative Solarz's experience is derived from an interview with a former member of his staff.

53. Congressional pressure concerning permission for the ROC to discuss the FX is documented in U.S. House of Representatives, *Implementation of the*

Taiwan Relations Act, p. 11. The 1981 letter was based on a hearing that examined, among other things, the ROC's defense needs. See U.S. Congress, House of Representatives, Committee on Foreign Affairs, Subcommittee on Asian and Pacific Affairs, *The New Era in East Asia: Hearings, May, June and July 1981* (Washington, D.C.: Government Printing Office, 1981), pp. 259–324. The letter concluded that the PRC had neither the capability nor the intention to mount an invasion of Taiwan and had political disincentives to doing so. The subcommittee received a reply from National Security Adviser Richard Allen, who was noncommittal on the subcommittee's policy conclusions. The subcommittee's letter to the president and Allen's reply are to be found in the subcommittee's files.

54. According to a former congressional aide who played a role in the drafting of the TRA, much effort had to be expended in reassuring Chairman Zablocki and Republicans that the TRA had solved the problem that normalization had created.

55. Interview with an informed observer of U.S. government arms sale decision making.

56. U.S. Senate, *U.S. Policy Toward China and Taiwan,* p. 22.

57. Ibid., p. 27.

58. Letter to President Reagan from members of the House Subcommittee on Asian and Pacific Affairs, p. 2.

59. *Beijing Review,* October 9, 1984.

60. *New York Times,* January 9, 1979.

61. Hu Yao-pang interview, *P'ai Hsing,* December 25, 1985.

62. Teng made his statement on September 2, 1986 on the CBS News program "60 Minutes." The radio broadcast is reported in *Foreign Broadcast Information Service, Daily Report: China* (hereafter *FBIS*), September 9, 1987, p. 42. Whether the broadcast reflects government policy may be open to some question.

63. U.S. Senate, *U.S. Policy Toward China and Taiwan,* p. 27.

64. Martin L. Lasater, *The Taiwan Issue in Sino-American Relations,* The Heritage Lectures, no. 49 (Washington, D.C.: Heritage Foundation, 1986), p. 3.

65. *New York Times,* October 12, 1984; Hu interview, *P'ai Hsing,* December 25, 1985.

66. *United Evening News* (Taipei), May 17, 1988. On the blockade option, see the interesting discussion in Martin L. Lasater (ed.), *Beijing's Blockade Threat to Taiwan,* The Heritage Lectures, no. 80 (Washington, D.C.: Heritage Foundation, 1986).

67. Oksenberg, "Sino-American Relations," p. 188.

68. U.S. Government Accounting Office report, p. 10.

69. Haig, *Caveat,* p. 204.

70. U.S. Senate, *U.S. Policy Toward China and Taiwan,* p. 19.

71. Lasater, *The Taiwan Issue in Sino-American Relations,* p. 5.

72. For reaction to the C-130 sale, see *FBIS,* June 21, 1984, pp. B2–B3.

73. U.S. Congress, House of Representatives, Committee on Foreign Affairs, Subcommittee on Asian and Pacific Affairs, *United States China Relations: Hearing* (Washington, D.C.: Government Printing Office, 1984), p. 231.

74. *Washington Post,* March 31, 1984.

75. Robert Karniol, "New Arms for Old," *Far Eastern Economic Review,* July 30, 1987, pp. 15–17. See also the companion articles "Home-Made Missiles" (p. 16) and "Taiwan's Warheads" (p. 18). Elements of Karniol's report have been confirmed in the Taiwan press and U.S. defense journals. A limited program of import substitution began on Taiwan in the wake of rapprochement between the United States and the PRC.

76. *Washington Post,* April 25, 1986.

77. Chang Ching-hsu, "A Preliminary Analysis of the 'Taiwan Straits's Military Power Balance' Theory," *Liaowang Overseas Edition,* July 28, 1986, pp. 22–23, translated in *FBIS,* August 1, 1986, pp. B2–B4.

78. Nayan Chanda, "A Technical Point," *Far Eastern Economic Review,* August 28, 1986, pp. 26–27.

79. A. Doak Barnett, *U.S. Arms Sales: The China-Taiwan Tangle* (Washington, D.C.: Brookings Institution, 1982), p. 69.

80. The most extensive and authoritative statement of the rationale and implementation of PRC arms sales policy is Edward Ross, "U.S.-China Military Relations," in Martin L. Lasater (ed.), *The Two Chinas: A Contemporary View* (Washington, D.C.: Heritage Foundation, 1986), pp. 83–90.

81. Martin L. Lasater, "Wanted: A U.S. Policy for Selling Arms to China," *Heritage Foundation Executive Memorandum,* no. 196 (January 15, 1986); M. Lasater, "Arming the Dragon: How Much U.S. Military Aid to China?" *The Heritage Lectures,* no. 53, March 1986.

82. *Congressional Record,* March 15, 1986, pp. S2957–S2958.

83. U.S. Congress, Senate, Committee on Foreign Relations, *Legislative Calendar (Cumulative Record): Ninety-Ninth Congress, December 31, 1986* (Washington, D.C.: Government Printing Office, 1986), p. 83.

84. U.S. Congress, House of Representatives, Committee on Foreign Affairs, Subcommittee on Asian and Pacific Affairs, *Implementation of the Taiwan Relations Act: Hearing* (Washington, D.C.: Government Printing Office, 1987), p. 43. The passage cited is from testimony by Representative Siljander at the May 7 session of the hearing in question. Had Representative Siljander desired, Representative Solarz, the chairman of the committee, would have held a public hearing on the avionics sale and held a vote on the resolution of disapproval. Neither was requested, however.

85. Selig S. Harrison, "Taiwan After Chiang Ching-kuo," *Foreign Affairs,* no. 66 (Spring 1988): 804–5.

86. Ibid., pp. 806–7.

87. Ibid., p. 791.

RALPH CLOUGH

The People's Republic of China and the Taiwan Relations Act

As early as 1950, the leaders of the People's Republic of China (PRC) believed that the United States wanted to separate Taiwan permanently from the Chinese mainland and keep it under its control. Despite U.S. recognition of the PRC as the legitimate government of China and U.S. acknowledgment of the Chinese view that Taiwan is part of China, they remained deeply suspicious of long-term U.S. intentions toward Taiwan. They attacked the Taiwan Relations Act (TRA), which they believed obstructed their efforts to impose their rule over Taiwan and eliminate the Republic of China (ROC).

In June 1950, President Harry S. Truman, following the outbreak of the Korean War, reversed his hands-off policy toward the ROC and ordered the Seventh Fleet to prevent its takeover. General Douglas MacArthur then visited the island, where he praised President Chiang Kai-shek for his resistance to communist aggression and declared that "the foundation for Sino-American military cooperation had been laid." In a message to the Veterans of Foreign Wars, he referred to Taiwan as "an unsinkable aircraft carrier," which the United States could not allow to become an enemy salient in the U.S. defense perimeter.[1]

PRC leaders, who had been preparing to invade Taiwan and seal their victory in the Chinese civil war, were outraged. Foreign Minister

Chou En-lai cabled the United Nations Security Council, charging that the intervention of the Seventh Fleet in the Taiwan Strait and the arrival of U.S. Air Force units in Taiwan was "direct armed aggression on Chinese territory."[2] On November 28, 1950, PRC representative Wu Hsiu-ch'uan, speaking before the U.N. Security Council, rejected President Truman's statement that the status of Taiwan was yet to be determined.[3]

Subsequent U.S. behavior during the 1950s and 1960s served to confirm the PRC's conviction that U.S. policy was to perpetuate the existence of two Chinese states. Washington gave the ROC hundreds of millions of dollars in military and economic aid. In December 1954, the United States signed a mutual security treaty with the ROC, which gave U.S. authorities the right to station forces in Taiwan. Shortly thereafter, Congress passed the Formosa Resolution, authorizing the president to employ U.S. forces in the defense of the offshore islands if he saw such intervention as essential to the defense of the ROC. The United States did not construct military bases in Taiwan comparable to those in Japan or the Philippines, but it stationed a Matador missile unit there in 1957, rotated U.S. Air Force units in and out of airfields in Taiwan, and invested $25 million to prepare Kung Kuan (now Ching Chuan Kang) Airfield for contingency use by U.S. aircraft. Statements by high U.S. officials frequently described the ROC as a vital link in the U.S. defense perimeter in the Western Pacific.

The PRC reacted strongly to the signing of the mutual security treaty between the United States and the ROC. "The U.S. government is trying by means of this treaty to legalize its armed seizure of the Chinese territory of Taiwan and make Taiwan a base for further aggression against China and the preparation for a new war," declared Chou En-lai. He warned that "all proposals to set up a so-called 'independent state' of Taiwan, to 'neutralize' Taiwan or to place Taiwan under 'trusteeship' mean in practice, dismemberment of China's territory, infringement upon China's sovereignty and interference in China's internal affairs. All are therefore utterly unacceptable to the Chinese people."[4]

At the ambassadorial-level talks between the United States and the PRC begun in Geneva in 1955, the PRC negotiator sought to draw a sharp line between the U.S. "occupation" of Taiwan, which he defined as an international issue, and the right of the PRC, as the legal government of China, to "liberate" Taiwan by either peaceful means or by force, which he defined as a domestic issue. He rejected U.S. insistence on renunciation of force in the Taiwan area as attempted interference in the PRC's domestic affairs. In subsequent official statements, the PRC repeatedly accused the United States of plotting to create "two Chinas" and of being a clandestine supporter of the Taiwan Independence Movement.[5]

The PRC used a variety of tactics in its efforts to put an end to U.S. protection of the ROC, including mobilization of international support for the PRC position, negotiation with the United States at the ambassadorial talks, offers of negotiation and threats of force aimed at the ROC, and, in 1958, the bombardment of Quemoy (Chinmen), the principal offshore island.

The U.S. reaction to the PRC's attempt to interdict the resupply of Quemoy demonstrated its determination to defend the ROC from the PRC. It provided new weapons to the ROC defenders and convoyed ROC supply ships to within three miles of Quemoy. In the ambassadorial talks at Warsaw, the United States proposed a ceasefire, to be followed by arrangements to demilitarize or neutralize the offshore islands. Alarmed by the tendency in many countries around the world to favor severing the offshore island link between Taiwan and the Chinese mainland, Beijing let it be known that its policy was to leave the ROC in possession of the offshore islands until Taiwan itself could be "liberated."

The PRC's control of the Chinese mainland placed it in a powerful position from which to steadily weaken the international status of the ROC by insisting on severance of relations with Taipei as the price for the establishment of relations with Beijing. Support for the admission of the PRC to the U.N. increased among member states. In 1971, the United States itself withdrew its objection to the admission of the PRC and failed to preserve a seat for the ROC. By this time, the United States had decided to establish a bilateral relationship with Beijing short of formal diplomatic relations.

Breakthrough, 1971–1973

Throughout the 1960s, the PRC had insisted in the ambassadorial talks that no progress could be made in U.S.-PRC relations until the Taiwan problem had been resolved. By the end of the decade, however, with prospects bright for ousting the ROC from the China seat in the U.N., the PRC changed its tactics, in the hope that negotiations with President Richard Nixon and his national security adviser, Henry Kissinger, would lead to progress on the Taiwan issue, even though not necessarily to its final resolution.

The result was the Shanghai communiqué of February 1972, in which the PRC restated its position that it was the sole legal government of China and that Taiwan was a province of China. The PRC leaders also declared that no state had a right to interfere with the liberation of Taiwan and demanded that all U.S. forces and military installations be withdrawn from the island. They expressed firm opposition to any activities that aimed to create "one China, one Taiwan," "one China, two governments," "two Chinas" or an "independent Taiwan."

The U.S. government went part way to meet the PRC's demands with the following declaration:

> The United States acknowledges that all Chinese on either side of the Taiwan Strait maintain that there is but one China and that Taiwan is part of China. The United States Government does not challenge that position. It reaffirms its interest in a peaceful settlement of the Taiwan question by the Chinese themselves. With this prospect in mind, it reaffirms the ultimate objective of the withdrawal of all U.S. forces and military installations from Taiwan. In the meantime, it will progressively reduce its forces and military installations on Taiwan as tension in the area diminishes.[6]

Although the United States did not agree in the Shanghai communiqué that Taiwan was a province of the PRC, it did not question the "one China" view held by both Beijing and Taipei. Thereafter, the U.S. dropped the assertion that sovereignty over Taiwan remained to be determined, an assertion that had been made by a State Department spokesman as late as April 1971.[7] The commitment to ultimately withdraw U.S. forces and military installations from Taiwan, although without a date for completing the withdrawal, was an important concession to a long-standing, basic PRC demand. From the PRC viewpoint, the risk that the United States would support an independent state of Taiwan had been significantly lessened.

The admission of the PRC to the U.N. and the rapprochement between Washington and Beijing greatly strengthened Beijing's position in the international community. In 1972, Japan recognized the government of the PRC as the sole legal government of China and broke relations with the ROC. Many other countries followed. The PRC replaced the ROC as the representative of China in most intergovernmental organizations. It was having increasing success in its drive to sever Taiwan's official relations with other states.

The PRC's agreement in 1973 to establish liaison offices in Beijing and Washington was a calculated gamble. It had never before maintained an official office in a place where the ROC had a full-fledged embassy. For five years, an officially sanctioned "two Chinas" arrangement existed in Washington. But the PRC had calculated, correctly, that the liaison office arrangement would help to bring about the normalization of diplomatic relations with the United States.

Normalization, 1978–1979

In the course of difficult negotiations, the United States finally accepted the PRC's three basic conditions for the establishment of diplomatic relations: the severance of diplomatic relations with the ROC, the ending of the security treaty, and the withdrawal of U.S. forces and military installations from Taiwan. In the joint communiqué on the establishment of diplomatic relations of December 15, 1978, the United States also recognized the PRC as "the sole legal government of China," stated that it would maintain "cultural, commercial, and other unofficial relations with the people of Taiwan," and inched closer to the PRC view on the status of Taiwan by declaring that it "acknowledged the Chinese position that there is but one China and Taiwan is part of China."[8]

The long-standing disagreement between the United States and the PRC concerning the latter's refusal to renounce the right to use force to destroy the ROC and the U.S. determination to supply the ROC with the means to defend itself was not resolved in the normalization negotiations. The United States informed the PRC that it would continue to sell defensive weapons to the ROC after the termination of the security treaty, and the PRC declared that it "absolutely would not agree to this." The dispute was set aside for later resolution.[9]

The PRC saw the normalization agreement as a crucial step toward its goal of gaining control over Taiwan. It had won U.S. recognition as the sole legal government of China and U.S. acknowledgment of its position that Taiwan was part of China. The United States had also agreed to withdraw its military forces and end its defense commitment. Having compelled the United States to drop its formal commitment to defend the ROC, the PRC promptly moved to take advantage of the ROC's more vulnerable situation.

In a message to "Taiwan compatriots" on New Year's Day 1979, the Standing Committee of the National People's Congress announced cessation of the odd-day shelling of the offshore islands and called for negotiations between the PRC and the ROC to end their military confrontation. Declaring that all conditions now favored reunification, the PRC message also proposed increased trade and travel and the establishment of transportation and postal services between Taiwan and the mainland. The message assured the people on Taiwan that PRC authorities would take realities into account, respect the opinions of the people on Taiwan, and adopt reasonable measures to settle the question of reunification, "so as not to cause the people of Taiwan any losses."[10] ROC authorities flatly rejected this PRC overture as a deceptive maneuver aimed at imposing the communist system on Taiwan.

Meanwhile, the U.S. Congress passed the TRA to govern relations between the United States and the ROC in the new situation. Members of Congress had included language in that bill to show continued U.S. concern for the ROC's security. The Act stated that the U.S. decision to establish diplomatic relations with the PRC rested on the expectation that the future of Taiwan would be determined by peaceful means. The Act went on to declare that "any effort to determine the future of Taiwan by other than peaceful means" would be considered "of grave concern to the United States." The Act further provided that the United States would supply the ROC with defensive arms and would maintain a capacity "to resist any resort to force or other means of coercion that would jeopardize the security or the social and economic system of the people of Taiwan." According to the Act, the nature and quantity of defense articles needed by Taiwan were to be determined solely by the president and the Congress of the United States.[11]

Initial PRC Reaction to
the Taiwan Relations Act

On March 16, 1979, just after the Senate and the House of Representatives had passed similar bills on future U.S. relations with Taiwan, but before Senate and House conferees had agreed on the language of the final bill, PRC Foreign Minister Huang Hua protested to Ambassador Leonard Woodcock that "if the bills are passed as they are worded now, and are signed into law, great harm will be done to the new relationship that has just been established between China and the United States."[12] The PRC particularly objected to the language that Congress had added to the administration's draft bill expressing U.S. concern with Taiwan's security and committing the United States to continue to supply defensive arms. Despite the protest, President Jimmy Carter signed the Act.

Shortly thereafter, when a delegation from the Senate Foreign Relations Committee headed by the committee chairman, Frank Church, visited Beijing, Deputy Prime Minister Teng Hsiao-p'ing told them that passage of the TRA had come close to nullifying the normalization of relations between the United States and China. He added that the United States should not be so concerned about an attack on Taiwan as the PRC would not have the capability for such an attack for five years and would use force against Taiwan only if the authorities there persisted in refusing to negotiate or if the Soviet Union became involved in Taiwan. Teng asserted that U.S. legislation authorizing continued arms sales had made the Taiwan authorities more stubborn in resisting negotiations.[13]

Despite their discomfiture at the defense-related language of the TRA, PRC leaders pressed ahead on a variety of fronts in expanding relations with the United States. They did not allow the continuing disagreement over Taiwan to stand in the way of strengthening a relationship they needed to counter the Soviet threat and to further China's development under the "Four Modernizations" program. Although they regarded the TRA as contravening the principles of the joint communiqué on normalization of relations, they probably took some comfort from President Carter's pledge when he signed the Act, that in administering it he would exercise presidential discretion in a manner consistent "with the understandings we reached on the normalization of relations with the People's Republic of China, as expressed in our Joint Communiqué."[14]

Growing Tensions
Over Taiwan

From mid 1980 until August 1982, the expanding relations between Washington and Beijing were threatened by an intensifying dispute over U.S. relations with the ROC. The dispute had two principal themes. The first consisted of statements and actions by the U.S. government and by influential individuals, particularly by presidential candidate Ronald Reagan, that tended to give a more official character to relations between Washington and Taipei. The second was the continued sale of military equipment to the ROC. The two themes were closely interrelated, for the PRC leaders felt that arms sales violated the U.S. pledge to have only unofficial relations with Taiwan. They took the view that "arms supply to the Taiwan authorities is completely different from the maintenance of normal commercial relations with the people of Taiwan."[15]

The PRC initially treated candidate Reagan's statement backing the re-establishment of official relations with the ROC as nothing more than "a little eddy" in the mainstream of smoothly developing Sino-U.S. relations.[16] By August 1980, however, the PRC took a more serious view of Reagan's repeated advocacy of official relations with the ROC and his reference to the TRA as a justification for his position. A *People's Daily* commentator, attacking Reagan's reliance on the TRA, pointed out that in his August 25 press conference he had made no mention at all of the joint communiqué on the establishment of diplomatic relations. The commentator declared that the TRA was a U.S. domestic law that in many places ran counter to the principles of the joint communiqué and could in no way serve as a legal basis for handling U.S.-Chinese relations.[17]

An agreement signed in October 1980 by the American Institute in Taiwan (AIT) and the Coordination Council for North American Affairs (CCNAA) granted diplomatic privileges and immunities to these organizations. The U.S. government endorsed that agreement, and the PRC reacted with anger. A *People's Daily* commentator argued that granting diplomatic privileges and immunities to these organizations accorded them official status. He again denounced the TRA and charged the U.S. government with "breaking its own commitment and going counter to the principles governing the establishment of diplomatic relations."[18]

After President Reagan's inauguration, he quickly backed away from his promise to re-establish official relations with Taiwan, but other influential Republicans continued to stress the importance of strengthening relations with Taiwan by strongly supporting the TRA. The PRC voiced its uneasiness over the intentions of the Reagan administration in an article in the *Guangming Ribao* on May 31, 1981. The article expressed three principal objections to the TRA:

- It flagrantly interferes in China's domestic affairs by expressing the U.S. intention to prevent any use of force to resolve the Taiwan problem;
- It stipulates continued sales of weapons to Taiwan, thus encouraging the Taiwan authorities' separatist tendencies and obstructing the peaceful reunification of the motherland; and

- It regards Taiwan as a "country" by specifying that U.S. laws applying to foreign countries or governments also apply to Taiwan and by giving diplomatic privileges and immunities to representatives of Taiwan.

The article "emphatically" pointed out that the TRA was a U.S. domestic law; therefore, as stipulated by the U.N. charter and the 1969 Vienna Convention on Treaties and Laws, that law could not override international agreements between countries.[19]

U.S. arms sales to the ROC soon became the central issue between Washington and Beijing.[20] At the time of Secretary of State Alexander Haig's visit to China in June 1981, the PRC sharply rejected the idea put forward by some U.S. leaders that the sale of U.S. weapons to the PRC would make it more tolerant of weapons sales to the ROC. An article in the *People's Daily* refuted the justifications based on the TRA for the continued supply of arms to the ROC. For the PRC, the article declared, it was a matter of principle that the United States had no right to supply weapons to Taiwan after recognizing the PRC as the sole legitimate government of China and Taiwan as part of China's territory.[21]

While the dispute between the United States and the PRC over arms sales continued to heat up, Beijing made another major overture to Taiwan. On September 30, 1981, Yeh Chien-ying, chairman of the Standing Committee of the National People's Congress, expanded the PRC's policy toward Taiwan in a nine-point proposal. In additon to calling for talks between the Chinese Communist Party and the KMT and reiterating earlier proposals for trade, travel, and communication, Yeh said that after reunification Taiwan would enjoy a high degree of autonomy as a special administrative region and could retain its armed forces, its socioeconomic system, its way of life, and its economic and cultural relations with foreign countries. The central government would not interfere in local affairs in Taiwan or encroach on rights to private property or foreign investments. Taipei promptly rejected the nine-point proposal, which President Chiang Ching-kuo characterized as "primarily intended to stop U.S. arms sales to our country."[22]

The dispute over arms sales increased tensions between the two countries. In early 1981, the PRC downgraded relations with the Netherlands from the ambassadorial to the charge d'affaires level because that country had sold two submarines to the ROC. Peking was "killing the chicken to warn the monkey." In February 1982, Teng Hsiao-p'ing told Prince Norodom Sihanouk that China was ready to downgrade its diplomatic relations with the United States. "Some people in America," Teng said, "think that Taiwan is their unsinkable aircraft carrier in the Far East. If this idea prevails, it is very difficult to build good Sino-American relations. The essence of this idea is to deny that Taiwan is a part of the People's Republic of China."[23]

A U.S. decision to reject the ROC's bid for a more advanced fighter aircraft failed to placate Beijing, for the United States agreed to continue the co-production of additional F-5E fighters for Taiwan's air force. The PRC declared that it would not be satisfied with anything short of a date for the termination of all U.S. arms sales to Taiwan. President Reagan sought to reassure the PRC in letters to Chao Tzu-yang, Teng Hsiao-p'ing, and Hu Yao-pang, in which he declared:

> (a) that the United States recognized only one China and that it would not permit the unofficial relations between the American people and the people of Taiwan to weaken its commitment to this principle;
>
> (b) that the United States recognized the significance of the PRC's policy toward Taiwan enunciated on January 1, 1979 and welcomed the nine-point proposal toward Taiwan made by Ye Jianying on September 30, 1981; and
>
> (c) that progress toward a peaceful solution of the Taiwan problem would naturally decrease the need for arms by Taiwan and that U.S. positioning during February and March 1982 reflected this view.[24]

The Reagan letters, which seemed to reject any U.S. support for the concept of an independent Taiwan more firmly than the Shanghai communiqué or the joint communiqué on the normalization of diplomatic relations, were followed by a visit by Vice-President George Bush to Beijing. Negotiations continued in a tense atmosphere.

To bolster its contention that the U.S. sale of arms to the ROC could not be justified by appealing to a U.S. domestic law, the PRC published an interview with Professor Ch'en T'i-ch'iang, vice-president of the Chinese Society of International Law. Professor Chen cited numerous U.S. authorities to the effect that international obligations entered into by a state had precedence over domestic legislation. Hence, Professor Chen argued, the TRA did not provide a valid justification for the United States to continue to sell weapons to Taiwan. He cited the arbitration in the Alabama Claims case, which compelled the British government to pay damages for having allowed a British firm to sell an armed vessel to the Confederate States during the Civil War despite the British proclamation of neutrality.[25]

In July 1982, the PRC expressed its growing irritation with the

United States by carrying in full in the *People's Daily* a lengthy article by a Chinese scholar quoting extensively from U.S. official documents of the 1948–1950 period to demonstrate that U.S. civilian and military officials had long harbored a desire to separate Taiwan from China.[26] According to the author, the United States had been compelled by the trend of events to adopt a short-term hands-off policy toward Taiwan in early 1950, but the United States promptly reverted to the policy of keeping Taiwan separate from China when the outbreak of the Korean War provided a convenient excuse. Even after the United States had recognized the PRC as the sole legal government of China and Taiwan as part of China, the article concluded, the adoption of the TRA meant that the United States was still unwilling to stop interfering in Chinese domestic affairs, a consequence of the historical "imperialist expansionist policy on the part of the United States."

The August 17, 1982, Communiqué

The fractious dispute over arms sales was eased, although not resolved, by an agreement announced in a communiqué on August 17, 1982.[27] Both sides made concessions, but the net result was to nudge the United States toward eventually ending weapons sales to the ROC.

The PRC dropped its demand for a date for the termination of U.S. arms sales. While reiterating that the Taiwan question was China's internal affair, it referred to the proposals to Taiwan of 1979 and 1982 as evidence of its "fundamental policy to strive for a peaceful solution of the Taiwan question."

The United States declared that it had "no intention of infringing on China's sovereignty and territorial integrity, or interfering in China's internal affairs, or pursuing a policy of 'two Chinas' or 'one China, one Taiwan.'" It expressed appreciation for the PRC's policy of striving for a peaceful resolution of the Taiwan question, in light of which it stated that the United States "does not seek to carry out a long-term policy of arms sales to Taiwan, that its arms sales to Taiwan will not exceed, either in quantitative or qualitative terms, the level of those supplied in recent years since the establishment of diplomatic relations between the United States and China, and that it intends to reduce gradually its sales of arms to Taiwan, leading, over a period of time, to a final resolution."

Statements by the two governments concerning the communiqué revealed striking differences between them on its interpretation. The

U.S. spokesmen asserted that the U.S. agreement to reduce arms sales gradually to the ROC was predicated on the continuation of China's peaceful policy toward the resolution of its differences with the ROC. Should the Chinese change this "fundamental" policy, the U.S. would re-examine its position. The spokesmen stressed that U.S. statements in the communiqué were fully consistent with the TRA.[28]

The Chinese spokesman rejected any interpretation of the communiqué linking it to the TRA. He interpreted the phrase "leading, over a period of time, to a final resolution" as implying the complete termination of U.S. arms sales to the ROC, and he expressed the hope that such a resolution could be achieved at an early date. He insisted that China's policy of striving for a peaceful resolution of the Taiwan question was an internal affair in which no foreign interference was permissible, thus implicitly rejecting the U.S. linkage of China's policy toward the ROC with U.S. policy toward arms sales.[29]

Although the PRC was not entirely satisfied with the agreement and expressed doubt that the United States would faithfully carry out its provisions, the agreement did represent further progress in the PRC's persistent effort to weaken U.S. support for the ROC and add to the pressure on the Taipei leadership to enter into negotiations with Beijing. Statements in the agreement suggested that the United States now approved of the reunification of Taiwan with China and did not support a Taiwan permanently severed from the government of the Chinese mainland.

In an effort to blunt the adverse effect on U.S.-ROC relations of the U.S.-PRC agreement on arms sales, the United States gave the following assurances to ROC leaders. The U.S. government:

- had not agreed to set a date for ending arms sales to the ROC;
- had not agreed to hold prior consultations with the PRC on arms sales to the ROC;
- would not play any mediation role between Taipei and Beijing;
- had not agreed to revise the TRA;
- had not altered its position regarding sovereignty over Taiwan; and
- would not exert pressure on ROC authorities to enter into negotiations with the PRC.[30]

Despite these assurances, the authorities and media in Taiwan denounced the agreement as highly damaging to the interests of the people of Taiwan.

Continuing Differences on Arms Sales and the Taiwan Relations Act

The Reagan administration's formal notification to Congress two days after the August 17 agreement that it intended to sell an additional 60 F-5E's to the ROC came as no surprise to the PRC and evoked no protest. The decision had been made public months before, but formal notification to the Congress had been withheld until an agreement on arms sales could be reached with Beijing. Thereafter, however, announcements of arms sales to the ROC regularly provoked protests by Beijing that the United States was exceeding either the quantity or the quality of weapons sold to the ROC in previous years, thus violating its agreement in the August 17 communiqué. For example, when Secretary of State George Shultz visited Beijing in February 1983, the Chinese complained that the ceiling set by the United States, from which reductions would be calculated, was much higher than sales announced by U.S. government departments in previous years. Shultz's comment that the sales were in accord with the TRA brought the retort that the TRA was a serious stumbling block in the way of Sino-U.S. relations and should be annulled.[31] About the same time, the Xinhua News Agency issued a strong objection to resolutions proposed in the House and Senate calling for the peaceful settlement of Taiwan's future to be consistent with laws enacted by the Congress and the communiqué between the United States and the PRC.[32]

When House Speaker Thomas P. ("Tip") O'Neill headed a congressional delegation to Beijing in March 1983, including Clement J. Zablocki, chairman of the House Foreign Affairs Committee, P'eng Chen, vice-chairman of the National People's congress, denounced the TRA for trying to turn Taiwan into "an unsinkable aircraft carrier." Zablocki told the press that in the meetings with Chinese officials, including Premier Chao Tzu-yang and Foreign Minister Wu Hsüeh-ch'ien, those officials repeatedly urged the repeal of the TRA.[33] A *China Daily* article published during the visit declared that "it is sheer mockery for the United States to profess interest in a peaceful reunification of Taiwan while militarily supporting the Taiwan authorities' intransigence in holding on to the status quo."[34] In July 1983, Chinese ambassador Chang Wen-chin lodged a strong protest at the U.S. announcement of plans to sell $530 million worth of arms to the ROC, charging that the planned sale exceeded the level of sales in recent years and that some of the missiles being supplied were more advanced than those already possessed by the ROC, thus contravening U.S. commitments in the August 17 communiqué.[35]

In subsequent years, Chinese officials regularly referred to the Taiwan issue as impeding the improvement of U.S.-PRC relations. For example, Chao Tzu-yang, in a televised press conference in January 1984 during his visit to the United States, said that the TRA was the essential obstacle that must be completely repealed in order to maintain steady and sustained development of U.S.-PRC relations. Chao conceded that the Congress was not inclined at that time to repeal the Act, but he said that China expected the U.S. government to strictly abide by the three communiqués.[36] Reports that U.S. companies were providing the ROC with the technology to produce an advanced fighter aircraft evoked criticism from the secretary-general of the Chinese Communist Party, Hu Yao-pang. The supply of military technology was not mentioned in the August 17 communiqué, but Hu contended that "arms sales and the transfer of technology for arms manufacture are the same thing."[37]

Chinese officials did not allow the United States to forget that the PRC opposed the TRA as intervention in China's domestic affairs and that the United States had bound itself to reduce and eventually end arms sales to the ROC. Statements regarding these PRC positions appeared in speeches and articles and in discussions between top-level officials of the two countries. Some of these statements also reflected various reactions to public controversy between the administration and its critics as to whether the U.S. government was adequately supplying the ROC with defensive weapons.

But disagreement over Taiwan did not again threaten to disrupt relations, as it had in 1981–1982. U.S.-PRC relations expanded and improved. Disputes arose over new issues, such as Tibet and the PRC's sale of missiles to the Persian Gulf states, but until mid 1988 the Chinese leaders seemed content to restate for the record their position on Taiwan without trying to wring further concessions from the United States on this issue.

The People's Republic of China and the Republic of China

The PRC's decision not to press the United States on the Taiwan issue might have been based on a judgment that no further concessions could be expected from the Reagan administration. That decision might also have been influenced by the increasing number of Chinese individuals and institutions that had developed a stake in the maintenance of good relations with the United States. But changes in the ROC and in that government's policy toward the PRC probably were the principal factors causing Beijing to follow a new, softer line on the Taiwan question.

Teng Hsiao-p'ing's concept of "one country, two systems," put forward in September 1982, introduced a new tactic for the takeover of Taiwan. In December 1982 this new concept was embodied in Article 31 of the fourth PRC constitution, which provided for special adminstrative regions designed to accommodate the Hong Kong, Macao, and Taiwan regions. When the PRC reached agreement with the British in September 1984 on the future of Hong Kong after 1997, Chinese officials took the occasion to renew offers to the ROC to have Taiwan become a special administrative region of the PRC, with even greater autonomy than that envisaged for Hong Kong. Teng Hsiao-p'ing had made clear, however, in an earlier discussion with a U.S. professor, that the autonomy planned for Taiwan would not be "complete autonomy," as that would mean "two Chinas." Taiwan would be a local government and only the PRC would be entitled to represent China in the international arena, Teng said.[38] The ROC authorities rebuffed these overtures, as they had earlier proposals, and showed no disposition to modify their policy of no contacts, no negotiations, and no compromise with the PRC.

In contrast to the ROC's official policy, however, contacts between individuals from Taiwan and the mainland increased steadily during the mid 1980s. Trade grew rapidly, surreptitious visits by people from Taiwan to relatives on the mainland occurred with increasing frequency, and many meetings took place between Chinese from Taiwan and the PRC in Hong Kong and elsewhere. The flow of information about Taiwan began to alter the simplistic view once held in Beijing that the mass of people on Taiwan were eager for unification under the PRC and that unification was prevented by only a few reactionary KMT leaders. Chinese officials and analysts recognized that people on Taiwan had understandable reasons for harboring misgivings about reunion with the mainland. They were confident that these misgivings could be overcome as economic and political reforms proceeded on the mainland and the people of Taiwan learned more about them, but they increasingly reconciled themselves to the probability that unification would be a long-term process.

As Chiang Ching-kuo aged, PRC officials and analysts began to express anxiety that his death would be followed by political chaos in the ROC, possibly even the seizure of power by Taiwanese extremists, who would declare an independent Taiwan Republic, thus compelling the PRC to use military force and thereby imperiling U.S.-PRC relations.[39] The emphasis on "self-determination" by a newly founded opposition party in the ROC, the Democratic Progressive Party, intensified this concern. When Chiang died, Chao Tzu-yang's message of condolence stressed the importance of "stability." Chinese officials called the attention of U.S. officials to this message, pointing out the importance of having political stability in Taiwan for both the PRC and the United States.

Although the PRC was concerned about the debate on self-determination for Taiwan and the growing influence of native Taiwanese in the ROC political system, PRC observers were encouraged by two developments that seemed to draw Taiwan closer to the mainland—the successful negotiations in May 1986 through unofficial channels for the return from Kuang-chou of a China Airlines plane and crew members taken there by a defecting pilot and Chiang Ching-kuo's decision in the fall of 1987 to allow people on Taiwan to visit their relatives on the mainland.

A better understanding by PRC officials of the complex attitudes in Taiwan toward the mainland, as well as an appreciation of differences in the United States on the Taiwan issue appeared to have influenced their view of how to deal with the United States on the ROC issue. To be sure, the PRC had not dropped its opposition to the TRA. On the contrary, Teng Hsiao-p'ing, when interviewed by CBS newscaster Mike Wallace in September 1986, reiterated his view that the TRA was "an immense obstacle in Sino-U.S. relations." But instead of attacking the United States for arms sales to Taiwan, Teng asked for some effort by the United States to promote China's reunification. He declared that "President Reagan, in particular, can accomplish something in regard to this question." Pressed to elaborate, he said that the United States could encourage and persuade the ROC to permit the exchange of mail, trade, and air and shipping services. Such contacts, Teng said, "can help enhance mutual understanding between the two sides of the Taiwan Straits, thus creating conditions for them to proceed to discuss the question of reunification and ways to achieve it."[40]

The breakthrough in unofficial contacts across the Taiwan Strait that occurred in 1987 resulted not from persuasion by the United States but from pressures on the ROC authorities by retired servicemen on Taiwan who wanted to see their relatives on the mainland before they died. Once the door opened, a flood of people poured into mainland China. By August 1988, nearly 150,000 had made the trip, and travel permits had been approved for an additional 50,000.[41] Although the great majority of such travelers visited their relatives, some used the trip for sightseeing or to make business deals. Historians and poets met with their professional mainland colleagues. Taiwan singers performed on the mainland, and artists exhibited their works. A delegation of members of the opposition Democratic Progressive Party even made the trip. A go champion from Taiwan competed in a world go tournament in Beijing. Three scientists from the Academia Sinica attended a meeting in Beijing of the International Council of Scientific Unions. Premier Yü Kuo-hua announced that student athletes from the ROC would be allowed to take part in international sports contests on the mainland.

Throughout 1988, Taiwan was in the grip of a "mainland fever." Pressures mounted for even fewer restrictions on mainland contacts. The new political pluralism on Taiwan had made the government more vulnerable to popular pressures. It gave ground little by little. Officials added twenty items to the list of products that could be imported from the mainland by indirect routes, and the first shipment of mainland coal arrived in Taiwan. Two-way trade was expected to reach $2.5 billion in 1988, as compared with $1.5 billion the previous year.[42] The government did not interfere with investments on the mainland by Taiwanese entrepreneurs. It even opened Taiwan's door a crack by announcing that it would permit residents of the mainland to visit Taiwan in the event of the grave illness or death of a close relative. Yet the authorities continued to maintain the three principles first advanced by the late President Chiang Ching-kuo that there be no contact, no negotiation, and no compromise on the part of officials with the PRC. An elderly KMT member of the Legislative Yuan, the 86-year-old Hu Ch'iu-yuan, was stripped of his party membership in September 1988 for defying the ban and meeting with senior officials in Beijing.

At the KMT Congress in July 1988, party elder Ch'en Li-fu and 33 colleagues proposed a long-term, low-interest loan of between $5 billion and $10 billion to the PRC if it would renounce the use of force against the ROC and abandon its four principles: Marxism-Leninism, the primacy of the Communist Party, the dictatorship of the proletariat, and the socialist system. Beijing expressed interest in Ch'en's proposal but ultimately rejected it on the grounds that the PRC could not abandon its principles. The excitement in the ROC over the expansion of unofficial links with the mainland and the new pressures on the ROC government to expand those links lessened the concern in the PRC over the possibility of a movement for Taiwan independence on the island.

PRC officials may feel that they have had some success in convincing the U.S. government of the advantages of contacts between the ROC and the PRC, for they have stressed the importance of Secretary Schultz's statement in Shanghai in February 1987 that the United States welcomed the indirect trade and human interchange between Taiwan and the mainland and that it would seek to foster an environment for such developments to continue. Perhaps the PRC leaders are beginning to realize that threatening to use force and pressing the United States to cut off arms sales weaken the position of those in Taiwan and the United States who favor closer relations between Taiwan and the mainland and strengthen the position of hard-line advocates of independence. PRC leaders are aware that many in the United States continue to stress the strategic importance of Taiwan to the United States, but PRC leaders also know that they share with many in the United States a strong desire to avoid military confrontation over Taiwan. Chinese policy makers may believe that in the present circumstances a soft policy on the Taiwan issue is best calculated to facilitate expanding relations between Taiwan and the mainland, to enlist the cooperation of the United States in encouraging this trend, and to keep open the possibility of eventual reunification.

Conclusions

The PRC's basic positions on Taiwan and U.S. relations with the ROC have remained unchanged. Motivated by nationalist feelings and a determination to restore China's territorial integrity, its goal is to assert its sovereignty over Taiwan and eliminate the ROC rule there. To the PRC, U.S. relations with the ROC continue to be an impediment to the attainment of this goal. The three communiqués represent partially successful attempts by the PRC to push the impediment aside, but the TRA, which PRC authorities regard as contravening positions in the communiqués, stands in the way. Consequently, they have repeatedly urged its repeal. They see the sale of U.S. weapons to the ROC as encouraging Taiwan's leaders not to negotiate with Beijing. Moreover, they have criticized the annual reduction in weapons delivery by the United States, as required by the

August 17 communiqué, as excruciatingly slow and even offset by the transfer of military technology to the ROC.

Although the PRC has not altered its basic positions toward Taiwan and U.S. relations with the ROC, it has modified its tactics. Since agreeing to the 1982 communiqué, the PRC's leaders have pursued a relatively soft policy toward the United States on the Taiwan issue. They have become more sophisticated in analyzing and responding to the diverse currents of opinion in the United States and the ROC. The growing trade and interchange between Taiwan and the mainland during the past several years have encouraged the continuation of this soft policy rather than reversion to threats against the ROC and pressures on the United States, as in the early 1980s.

The PRC's leaders believe the tide is running in the right direction. The channels of communication being created by trade and investment and innumerable private contacts have improved the climate for future negotiations with the ROC on reunification. The PRC authorities have taken steps to encourage this trend—steps referred to in Taiwan's press as a "peace offensive." As long as this policy produces the desired results—closer relations between people on both sides of the Taiwan Strait—the PRC's leaders can disregard the TRA and the U.S. policy of arming the ROC. Emphasis on these issues merely creates uneasiness in the ROC and slows the favorable trend currently under way.

Looking to the future, however, the possibility of a shift by Beijing back to a hard line cannot be ruled out. It could be a test of the new Bush administration on the Taiwan issue or, more likely, a response to developments in the PRC and the ROC. For example, if Beijing's economic reforms suffer severe setbacks, with adverse repercussions on Taiwan's mainland trade and investment, the economic incentives to promote mainland connections would be weakened. The mistreatment on the mainland of a few visitors from Taiwan could harm prospects for closer relations. In such circumstances, the "mainland fever" in the ROC might be superseded by vigorous demands for self-determination, causing the PRC to take action to halt the drift away from reunification. A change in international conditions, such as a marked improvement in Sino-Soviet relations and a cooling of U.S.-PRC relations, could make the PRC more willing to risk damage to its relations with the United States by a new test of strength over Taiwan.

Notes

1. Foster Rhea Dulles, *American Foreign Policy Toward Communist China, 1949–1969* (New York: Thomas Crowell, 1972), p. 100.

2. Hungdah Chiu (ed.), *China and the Question of Taiwan* (New York: Praeger, 1973), pp. 231–32.

3. Ibid., p. 234.

4. Chiu, *China and the Question of Taiwan,* pp. 253 and 256.

5. See, for example, "A Brief Account of the U.S. Two Chinas Plot," (*People's Daily,* August 7, 1961), in Chiu, *China and the Question of Taiwan,* pp. 312–17, and "U.S.-Japanese Reactionaries Step Up 'Taiwan Independence Movement' Plot," (*People's Daily,* February 24, 1970), in Chiu, pp. 335–38.

6. Ralph N. Clough, *Island China* (Cambridge, Mass.: Harvard University Press, 1978), p. 250.

7. Chiu, *China and the Question of Taiwan,* p. 340.

8. Lester L. Wolff and David L. Simon, eds., *Legislative History of the Taiwan Relations Act* (Jamaica, N.Y.: American Association for Chinese Studies, 1982), p. 305.

9. Charles W. Freeman, Jr., "The Princess of Rapprochement: Achievements and Problems," in Gene T. Hsiao and Michael Witunski (eds.), *Sino-American Normalization and Its Policy Implications* (New York: Praeger, 1983), p. 16 and appendix B, p. 245.

10. Robert L. Downen, *To Bridge the Taiwan Strait* (Washington, D.C.: Council for Social and Economic Studies, 1984), pp. 104–7.

11. Text of the Act is in Wolff and Simon, *Legislative History of the Taiwan Relations Act,* pp. 288–95.

12. *Washington Post,* March 25, 1979; *Beijing Review,* no. 13 (March 30, 1979), p. 8.

13. *New York Times,* April 20, 1979.

14. Hsiao and Witunski, *Sino-American Normalization,* p. 476.

15. *Foreign Broadcast Information Service, People's Republic of China* (cited hereafter as *FBIS*), June 23, 1980, p. B2.

16. *Beijing Review,* no. 25 (June 23, 1980), p. 8.

17. *FBIS,* August 28, 1980, pp. B1–B2.

18. *Beijing Review,* no. 42 (October 20, 1980), pp. 9–10.

19. *FBIS,* June 1, 1981, pp. B1–B3. The U.S.-PRC communiqués are not treaties, however, and the assertion that they legally override the TRA is questionable. See Terry Emerson, *What Determines U.S. Relations with China: The TRA or the August 17 Communiqué with Beijing?* (Washington, D.C.: Heritage Foundation, November 30, 1987).

20. For a detailed discussion of this issue, see A. Doak Barnett, *U.S. Arms*

Sales: The China-Taiwan Tangle (Washington, D.C.: Brookings Institution, 1982).

21. *Beijing Review,* no. 25 (June 22, 1981), pp. 11–12.

22. Downen, *To Bridge the Taiwan Strait,* p. 49. The full text of Yeh's proposal is in the appendix, pp. 104–7.

23. *New York Times,* March 27, 1982, quoting from the March issue of *Liaowang.*

24. For texts of the letters, see Hsiao and Witunski, *Sino-American Normalization,* pp. 277–80.

25. "U.S. Arms Sales to Taiwan Violate International Law," *Beijing Review,* no. 6 (February 8, 1982), pp. 11–14. See also the sources in Note 19.

26. Tzu Chung-yun, "U.S. Policy Toward Taiwan (1948–50)." See the slightly abridged version in *Beijing Review,* July 5, 1982, pp. 15–28 and July 12, 1982, pp. 22–25. Tzu, who did research on U.S. policy toward China in the United States, was, as of July 1988, the deputy director of the Institute of American and Canadian Studies, Chinese Academy of Social Sciences.

27. Text of communiqué in *New York Times,* August 18, 1982.

28. Statements by President Reagan and Assistant Secretary of State John Holdridge, in Hsiao and Witunski, *Sino-American Normalization,* pp. 286–92.

29. Statement by Chinese Foreign Ministry spokesman, ibid., pp. 285–86.

30. Martin L. Lasater, *The Taiwan Issue in Sino-American Strategic Relations* (Boulder, Colo.: Westview press, 1984), p. 210.

31. *Beijing Review,* no. 7 (February 14, 1983), pp. 8–9.

32. *Japan Times,* March 14, 1983.

33. *Washington Post,* March 30, 1983.

34. *Washington Post,* March 31, 1983.

35. *Beijing Review,* no. 31 (August 1, 1983), p. 8.

36. *Beijing Review,* no. 4 (January 23, 1984).

37. Interview with Selig Harrison, April 23, 1986, reported in the *Washington Post,* April 25, 1986.

38. Interview with Dr. Winston L. Y. Yang, *FBIS,* August 1, 1983, pp. V1-V2.

39. Tzu Chung-yun and Chuang Ch'u-p'ing, "Sino-U.S. Relations: Opportunities and Potential Crises," *Beijing Review,* no. 41 (October 14, 1985), pp. 21–24. The appearance of this article coincided with Vice-President George Bush's visit to Beijing, causing observers to think that the PRC was turning up the pressure on the United States over Taiwan, but in Bush's conversations top Chinese officials treated the Taiwan issue in a low-key fashion.

40. *Beijing Review,* no. 38 (September 22, 1986), p. 5.

41. *Free China Journal,* August 22, 1988.

42. *Free China Journal,* September 29, 1988.

DAVID CHOU

The Republic of China and the Taiwan Relations Act

ON DECEMBER 15, 1978, President Jimmy Carter broke U.S. diplomatic relations with the Republic of China (ROC) and established diplomatic relations with the People's Republic of China (PRC). He declared that, from January 1, 1979, "the American people and the people of Taiwan will maintain commercial, cultural, and other relations without government representation and without diplomatic relations."[1] To facilitate those unofficial relations between the ROC and the United States, the U.S. Congress enacted the Taiwan Relations Act (TRA), which was signed into law by President Carter in April 1979. It is a unique arrangement in the annals of world diplomatic history. No other country ever derecognized another country and then by legislation maintained with the unrecognized country a relationship unofficial in name but official in substance.

How has the ROC government responded to the implementation of the TRA by the Carter and Reagan administrations? The ROC government reacted to the TRA with general approval, partly because it was in line with the objectives of the ROC, and partly because it was a vast improvement over the Taiwan Omnibus Bill proposed by the Carter administration.

The Republic of China's
Five Principles

The ROC's objectives for guiding future U.S.-ROC relations in the absence of formal diplomatic relations were outlined in the five principles proposed by President Chiang Ching-kuo on December 29, 1978 to Deputy Secretary of State Warren Christopher. These five principles related to security, continuity, reality, legality, and governance.[2] The first principle required maintaining the security of the Asian-Pacific region in order to guarantee the security and livelihood of the people on Taiwan. The PRC was perceived by many ROC officials to be a persistent threat to Taiwan. The United States had been the ROC's major ally against that threat, and so it was only natural that ROC leaders worried about the security of Taiwan after the United States broke diplomatic ties with the ROC and terminated the mutual defense treaty of 1954. President Chiang maintained that, in order to ensure the peace and security of the Western Pacific, which included the security of the ROC, the United States must take concrete and effective measures to pledge its support to the countries in the region.

The principle of continuity involved the ROC's wish to maintain cultural, economic, trade, scientific, technological, and travel relations with the United States. The ROC wanted not only to continue these ties at their current levels but also to expand them in the future.

The principle of reality considered the ROC's role in the international community. President Chiang said that the international status of the ROC as an independent and sovereign state could not be changed merely because some countries established diplomatic ties with the PRC. The legal status and character of the ROC existed, and the United States must recognize and respect that fact.

The principle of legality sought to maintain the existing 60 treaties and agreements, as well as other arrangements, between the ROC and the United States. The Carter administration declared that, except for the mutual defense treaty of 1954, the treaties and agreements between the ROC and the United States would continue to be in force. President Chiang suggested that both countries take appropriate legislative measures to provide a legal basis for maintaining these treaties and agreements.

The principle of governance aimed at establishing government-to-government mechanisms for handling exchange and communications.

President Chiang pointed out that the complex interests of both countries made it impossible for them to be carried out by any private organization or individual.

In the talks held both in Taipei and in Washington, Carter administration officials insisted that the United States could maintain only unofficial relations with the people of Taiwan, that it would set up a private organization to handle the relations, and that it could not recognize the ROC either de jure or de facto. Because of such intransigence, the ROC government failed in the first round to achieve most of its objectives.

The Taiwan Relations Act

On January 26, 1979, the Carter administration submitted to the Congress the Taiwan Omnibus Bill, which was designed to provide the framework for maintaining "cultural, commercial, and other unofficial relations with the people of Taiwan."[3] However, most members of Congress believed that the bill was inadequate for ensuring the well-being of the people on Taiwan, and Congress decided to rewrite the bill. Consequently, Congress made changes to eliminate questions and ambiguities concerning trade and legal and economic issues. It also defined and strengthened the future U.S. commitment to the defense of the ROC. Through this new bill, the Taiwan Relations Act (TRA), the ROC achieved some of the objectives it had failed to achieve in its initial negotiations with the Carter administration.

U.S. Security Commitments to the Republic of China

The story of the TRA does not need to be repeated here.[4] Yet, a few significant points should be mentioned. In the negotiations for establishing diplomatic relations between Washington and Beijing, the Carter administration failed to obtain a "no-force" pledge from the PRC.[5] Carter seemed to believe that U.S. concern for the ROC's security, linked with some political and military constraints on Beijing, would be enough to deter the PRC from attacking Taiwan. In his televised speech of December 15, 1978, President Carter said, "The U.S. is confident that the people of Taiwan face a peaceful and prosperous future. The U.S. continues to have an interest in the peaceful resolution of the Taiwan issue and expects that the Taiwan issue will be settled peacefully by the Chinese themselves."[6] However, the Taiwan Omnibus Bill never mentioned any U.S. concern for Taiwan's security.

Members of Congress worried about the absence of any provisions in the proposed bill to protect the ROC. They proposed a security clause, which became Section 2 of the TRA, that declared that peace and stability in the Western Pacific area, including Taiwan, are "in the political, security, and economic interests of the U.S., and are matters of international concerns"; that the U.S. decision to establish diplomatic relations with the PRC "rests upon the expectation that the future of Taiwan will be determined by peaceful means"; that the U.S. will "consider any effort to determine the future of Taiwan by other than peaceful means, including by boycotts or embargoes, a threat to the peace and security of the Western Pacific area and of grave concern to the U.S."; that the U.S. would "provide Taiwan with arms of a defensive character"; and that the U.S. would maintain a sufficient capacity to "resist any resort to force or other forms of coercion that would jeopardize the security, or the social or economic system, of the people on Taiwan."[7]

The TRA made very clear that the United States would oppose PRC military or other coercive actions against Taiwan and did not regard the solution of the so-called Taiwan problem as purely a domestic matter for the PRC. Yet, although the TRA expresses "grave concern" regarding Taiwan's security, it does not specifically commit the United States to defend Taiwan.

The White House relented and allowed Congress to have the security clause for its bill, but it objected to any language that might commit the United States to provide the same aid as stated in the 1954 mutual defense treaty or that would directly link the security of the United States with that of the ROC. Senator Jacob K. Javits drafted an amendment to formally commit the United States to the protection of Taiwan in the event of an attack by the PRC.[8] Senator Charles Percy submitted an amendment stating that the United States would consider any effort to resolve the Taiwan issue by other than peaceful means as a threat to the peace and security of the Western Pacific and to the security of the United States.[9] During a House floor debate, Representatives Ken Kramer and Robert J. Lagomarsino introduced similar amendments.[10] These amendments, however, were defeated by White House lobbying.

The American Institute in Taiwan

A main feature of the Carter administration's bill was the establishment of the American Institute in Taiwan (AIT). The AIT was to be under the jurisdiction of the State Department and would serve as an unofficial liaison with the ROC. However, the Congress refused to use the term *unofficial* in the TRA for referring to relations between Washington and Taipei. That term was used only in the Taiwan Omnibus Bill. The Congress made a special effort to delete references to official and unofficial categories. The White House did not oppose that effort, but it threatened to veto any legislation that would restore formal government-to-government relations between the ROC and the United States.

During the debate to draft the TRA, all proposals involving formal official relations between the United States and the ROC were rejected. For example, Senator Gordon Humphrey submitted an amendment that would elevate the U.S. presence in Taiwan to the status of a "liaison office." The Senate rejected it by a vote of 57–37. Opponents of the amendment said that it violated the agreement reached between Washington and Beijing. On a 62–33 vote, the Senate rejected an amendment by Senator Robert Dole that would refer to "Taiwan" rather than to "the people on Taiwan" throughout the bill. Opponents said it would come too close to creating official relations between the United States and Taiwan.[11] The same fate befell the following proposals: an amendment by Representative John M. Ashbrook placing employees of the AIT on the U.S. government payroll; an amendment by Representative Gerald B. Solomon establishing consular relations between Washington and Taipei; an amendment by Representative William E. Dannemeyer for conducting relations through a "quasi-governmental" agency called "the U.S. Commission in Taiwan"; and an amendment by Representative George Hansen deleting the requirement that the U.S. agency in Taiwan be nongovernmental.[12]

Many of the battles the White House lost in the House or the Senate were later won in the House-Senate Conference Committee. The Committee eliminated or softened most provisions in the bills that were passed by the House and Senate that were opposed by the White House. Administration lobbyists wanted the bill to keep relations with Taiwan on a strictly unofficial basis. Major provisions opposed by the administration and modified by the conferees were: (1) the title of the House bill "U.S.-Taiwan Relations Act" was changed to the "Taiwan

Relations Act," and (2) the reference in the House bill to the performance of "consular duties" by employees of the new unofficial agency was replaced by a reference to the duties "as if" they were consular functions.

The Status of the Republic of China

Having recognized the PRC, the Carter administration tended to regard the ROC on Taiwan as a nonentity. However, the TRA specifically guarantees the legal status of Taiwan in U.S. domestic law and in fact treats it as a sovereign state. Under the TRA, Taiwan has the capacity to sue and be sued in U.S. courts. Whenever the laws of the United States refer or relate to foreign countries or governments, such terms shall include and such laws shall apply with respect to Taiwan. The absence of diplomatic relations would not affect in any way rights or obligations of Taiwan under the laws of the United States. The TRA also provides that any legal requirements for the maintenance of diplomatic relations with the United States shall not apply to, or be a bar to, ROC participation in activities of any kind under U.S. domestic laws.

Finally, the TRA provides Taipei and Washington with effective means to interact. For example, the president and the Congress would jointly determine the nature and quantity of arms and services needed to meet the requirements of the ROC's security. The president should "inform the Congress promptly of any threat to the security of the social or economic system of the people on Taiwan and any danger to the interest of the U.S. arising therefrom" (Section 3).[13] The dealings of the U.S. government with "the people on Taiwan" would be conducted through the AIT, which is specially authorized to enter into, carry out, and enforce agreements and arrangements with the ROC, and which in fact acts like an embassy (Section 6). In response to the provision of the TRA, the ROC also set up a corresponding "unofficial" body, the Coordination Council for North American Affairs (CCNAA).

Implementation of the Taiwan Relations Act During the First Decade

The TRA stipulates the guiding principles for maintaining U.S.-ROC relations and authorizes the president "to prescribe such rules and regulations as he may deem appropriate to carry out the purposes of the TRA" (Section 13).[14] Hence, the effective implementation of the TRA rests largely on the good faith of the executive branch. The Congress is provided with authority to see that the executive branch fully and faithfully complies with the Act.

The Negative Attitude of the Carter Administration

During the last two years of the Carter administration, U.S.-ROC relations were cool and tense. The ROC government was groping for a new formula and adjusting to increasingly unfriendly actions by the Carter administration.

Because Congress drafted the TRA over the objections of the Carter administration, that administration was unenthusiastic about faithfully implementing the TRA. When signing the TRA into law, President Carter said that Congress had wisely granted discretion to him and that he "will exercise that discretion in a manner consistent with our interest, in the well-being of the people on Taiwan, and with the understandings we reached on the normalization of relations with the PRC."[15] Carter's intention was to implement the TRA as he saw fit and not strictly according to the letter and spirit of the Act to satisfy Congress's concerns. Indeed, the Carter administration presented Congress with a series of faits accomplis that ran counter to both the letter and spirit of the TRA. Terminating the air transport agreement between the United States and the ROC was a prime example.

Signed in Nanking in 1946, the air transport agreement between the United States and the ROC was a contract that the TRA specifically guaranteed should be kept in force. Prior to enacting the TRA, the Carter administration frequently stated that the air transport agreement would continue to be in force. During hearings on the TRA, Senator Richard Stone asked how the State Department plan, following normalization with Beijing, would honor the various treaties and agreements with the ROC. Deputy Secretary of State Warren Christopher said that all international agreements would remain in force, except for the mutual defense treaty and related agreements, which would be terminated on January 1, 1980.[16]

Yet, within six months of the passage of the TRA, the Carter administration began to have second thoughts about honoring agreements with the ROC. The administration wanted a formal treaty for air transport rights between the United States and the PRC. According to testimony from Assistant Secretary of State Richard Halbrooke,

Beijing had specified that, to get this treaty, the United States had to terminate any similar agreement between the United States and the ROC.

The Carter administration advanced two arguments to defend its action. First, the air transport agreement was inappropriate and a hindrance to concluding an air transport agreement between Washington and Beijing. Christopher said: "The old Nanking agreement with Taiwan . . . covered the entire mainland China. It was outdated in its form; it was outdated in its concept; it simply was so behind the time that it needed to be revised."[17] The air transport agreement was amended by agreement in 1950 and 1969 to apply only to the territory of Taiwan. The United States could have entered into an air transport agreement with Beijing without terminating the air transport agreement with the ROC. As Senator Stone asserted:

> Where the entire agreement is clearly outmoded and wrong, you would have to terminate it. In this particular case, the aviation agreement is not entirely outmoded and wrong. Some provisions of it relate to the mainland, and I quite understand that you would want to delete those in further agreements . . . But this is not to say that the aviation agreement by its own terms has to be cancelled . . . [18]

Furthermore, the TRA permits termination of existing agreements. Referring to Section 4(c) of the TRA, Christopher argued that Congress must have recognized that some of the existing agreements would be terminated, otherwise the provision was a nullity.[19] Although Christopher was correct on legal grounds, morally and politically he was wrong because a few months earlier he had promised the Committee on Foreign Relations that all former agreements would remain in force.

Whatever merit administration arguments might have, they were merely ex post facto rationalizations to improve U.S. relations with the PRC. The Carter administration insisted on terminating the air transport agreement because otherwise Beijing would not agree to start negotiations on an air transport agreement with the United States. The readiness of the administration to break its promise to the ROC for the sake of placating Beijing was a test case. If the administration was not going to respect its traditional commitments, the TRA was not worth the paper it was written on. This incident naturally worried the ROC. As Chang King-yuh said: "The ROC sought to be assured that the way the U.S. proposed to terminate the Nanking agreement did not create a model for handling other agreements."[20]

Many members of Congress were not convinced that it was necessary to terminate the air transport agreement and replace it by an informal one, but they did not try to reverse the administration's decision. As Senator Glenn said: "This is up to the State Department to determine"[21] whether to terminate the agreement or not. The Senate Subcommittee on East Asian and Pacific Affairs obtained only a pledge from the Carter administration that the termination of the air transport agreement would not set a precedent for handling other agreements with the ROC.

Continuity Under the Reagan Administration

The Reagan administration at first gave many the impression that it intended to modify its predecessor's China policy. Several reasons created that impression. During the presidential campaign in 1980, Reagan had severely criticized Carter for betraying the ROC and hinted that he intended to restore U.S.-ROC relations to an official level. High party and governmental officials of the ROC were invited to participate in his inauguration ceremony, in spite of protests from Beijing. In addition to President Reagan, several high officials in his administration were known to be sympathetic to the ROC. ROC representatives were frequently received in U.S. government offices, even in the White House.[22] However, the new administration soon took steps that dashed any hopes of a genuine, substantive change in Washington's policy toward the ROC. ROC government officials who had been invited as guests to the presidential inauguration ceremony were not reinvited. Responding to Beijing's complaints, the Reagan administration changed its policy of allowing CCNAA officials direct access to the U.S. government.[23]

Although Reagan had given personal assurances of U.S. friendship and support to Taipei, the Reagan administration did not abandon all the practices of its predecessor, even when they had no basis in the TRA. For example, the United States still prohibits ROC military officers above the rank of major from receiving professional training in the United States. The U.S. Air Force plane that takes congressional delegations to Taipei then immediately flies to Okinawa or Hong Kong for an overnight stay so as not to be defined as an official contact with the ROC.

In some respects, however, the Reagan administration did implement the TRA more faithfully than the Carter administration. The TRA provides that the United States should not exclude Taiwan from membership in any international financial institutions or international organizations (Section 4d). The Carter administration caved in when the International Monetary Fund and the World Bank decided to expel the ROC to allow Beijing's entry into the two organizations. The Reagan administration demonstrated its sincerity in implementing the TRA by supporting the ROC's membership in the Asian Development Bank (ADB). In February 1983, Beijing asked to join the ADB but demanded that the ADB first oust the ROC. A month later, the State Department welcomed Beijing's decision to join the ADB, but it warned that any move to expel the ROC from the ADB would adversely affect continued U.S. support for the bank.[24] In view of Washington's strong opposition, Beijing gave up its attempt to change the ROC's status in the ADB and demanded only that the ROC's name be changed to "Taipei, China."

Before 1979, the ROC had fourteen offices functioning as consuls in the United States. The TRA provides that the president shall allow the ROC to establish the same number of offices that were operated in the United States before 1979. The Carter administration allowed only nine offices of the CCNAA to operate. The Reagan administration agreed to three more CCNAA offices: one in Boston, another in Kansas, and the third in Miami.

Arms Sales Under the Reagan Administration

The Carter administration imposed a one-year moratorium on arms sales to Taipei throughout 1979, although the 1954 mutual defense treaty remained in force during that year. The moratorium was imposed as a concession to Beijing's demand during the negotiations that all U.S. military contracts with the ROC be terminated. During 1979, however, the United States delivered $598 million of military equipment already contracted for by the ROC. On January 3, 1980, the Carter administration announced an arms sales contract with the ROC totalling $287 million, but it rejected Taipei's request for several sophisticated defense weapons, such as advanced jet fighters and naval Harpoon missiles. The Carter administration's reluctance to sell these weapons was largely due to worry about adverse reactions from Beijing. Even so, the TRA drafters had intended that arms sales to the ROC should continue despite Beijing's concerns. This prompted several members of the Senate Committee on Foreign Relations to send a letter to President Carter urging him to provide the ROC with advanced jet fighters like the FX aircraft.[25] In June 1980, President Carter authorized Northrop and General Dynamics to conduct preliminary discussions with the ROC, as well as other potential foreign

customers, to sell the FX aircraft.[26] But the Carter administration
never endorsed such a sale. For FY 1981, the Carter administration
approved only $295 million in arms sales to the ROC, and it rejected
all other ROC requests for defensive weapons and equipment.

Although President Reagan reiterated in his 1980 campaign
speeches his concerns about the ROC's security, he did not respond
quickly to the request of the ROC for arms sales. It was not until
December 28, 1981 that the State Department approved a request for
$97 million for spare parts by Taipei. The Reagan administration had
responded slowly to such requests because of pressure from Beijing.
Beijing had tolerated continued arms sales by the Carter administration, but by mid 1981 the PRC had made arms sales to the ROC an
issue of serious controversy between Washington and Beijing. Why
had Beijing changed its attitude on the issue of arms sales?

First, the PRC blamed the United States for its own failure to re-
unify Taiwan with mainland China. The PRC leaders had perhaps
hoped that after the normalization of relations the United States
would gradually abandon the ROC, thus making it possible for the
PRC to increase pressure on Taipei's leaders to open a dialogue with
Beijing. The TRA, however, reconfirmed the U.S. commitment to
Taiwan's security. The ROC had naturally rejected Beijing's nine-
point proposal for reunification. Beijing's leaders obviously feared that
continuation of the status quo in the Taiwan Strait could lead to the
permanent separation of Taiwan from the mainland. Therefore, they
wanted all U.S. arms sales to the ROC ended entirely. As A. Doak
Barnett said, however, even if Carter had been elected to a second
term, arms sales to the ROC would have become a serious issue in
U.S.-PRC relations.[27]

Second, Reagan's campaign speeches created apprehension in the
PRC. The PRC leaders worried about future U.S. policy toward the
ROC. They probably adopted this new, tough political position to
test the intentions of the Reagan administration.

Third, the PRC leaders were re-evaluating their policy toward the
two superpowers and were trying to adopt a more balanced policy
toward each of them.

Whatever the real cause of the arms sale controversy, Beijing increased its pressure on Washington. In early July 1981, the Foreign
Ministry warned the U.S. ambassador to Beijing, Arthur W. Hummel, Jr., that, if the United States continued to sell arms to the ROC,
Beijing would take unspecified strong action "with grave consequences for the strategic situation."[28] In August 1981, the PRC postponed indefinitely the planned visit by Liu Hua-ch'ing, deputy chief of

staff of the People's Liberation Army. In October, Beijing's foreign minister Huang Hua told Secretary Haig that the United States should specify the period of time during which it would sell arms to Taiwan and that those sales should decline year by year and then cease.[29]

In January 1982, the Reagan administration rejected Taipei's request for advanced aircraft but extended current co-production and sales of F-5E jet fighters to the ROC. The only reason for rejecting the request, as State Department spokesman Alan B. Romberg explained, was that officials of the State and Defense Departments and other agencies concerned with national security had concluded that no sale of advanced aircraft to Taiwan was required because no military need for it existed. This was debatable. But one thing was certain: Congress never participated in the discussions that led to the administration's decision. Meanwhile, Assistant Secretary of State John Holdridge went to Beijing to resolve the controversy. President Reagan was prepared to take a tough stance toward Beijing, but Haig somehow persuaded him to accommodate Beijing's request. Haig stressed the importance of the strategic relationship between Washington and Beijing and warned Reagan of possible political damage for the coming 1984 election if he refused to find a compromise with Beijing on this issue.[30]

The 1982 Communiqué

President Reagan accepted Haig's advice, and his administration issued the famous U.S.-PRC joint communiqué on August 17, 1982. The communiqué contained parallel statements of policy by Beijing and Washington. Beijing confirmed its "fundamental policy to strive for a peaceful solution to the Taiwan problem." The United States stated:

> Having in mind the foregoing statements of both sides, the United States government states that it does not seek to carry out a long-term policy of arms sales to Taiwan, that its arms sales to Taiwan will not exceed, either in qualitative or in quantitative terms, the level of those supplied in recent years since the establishment of diplomatic relations between the United States and [Communist] China, and that it intends to reduce gradually its sales of arms to Taiwan, leading over a period of time to a final resolution.[31]

The communiqué did not take the ROC by surprise. During discussions on the communiqué, the Reagan administration kept the

ROC informed of all developments. The ROC strongly opposed the communiqué, arguing that it violates both the letter and spirit of the TRA, and, more important, it imposes limits on arms sales to Taipei that are unnecessary and detrimental to Taiwan's security. By gradually reducing arms sales to the ROC, and with Beijing modernizing its large military forces, the military balance in the Taiwan Strait would shift irreversibly to the PRC's favor and place the ROC's national defense in great danger. To offset any such crisis, the ROC began to intensify its efforts to become self-sufficient in national defense while continuing to seek arms from the United States. The ROC now plans to produce its advanced jet fighter by the mid 1990s.

Prior to the communiqué, the Reagan administration gave Taipei six assurances. It pledged not to (1) set a date for ending arms sales to the ROC, (2) hold prior consultations with Beijing on arms sales to the ROC, (3) play any mediation role between Taipei and Beijing, (4) revise the TRA, (5) alter its position regarding sovereignty over Taiwan, or (6) exert pressure on the ROC to enter into negotiations with Beijing.[32]

The communiqué purported to solve the dispute over U.S. arms sales to the ROC, but, after the communiqué, differences in interpretation of its provisions immediately surfaced. In testimony before the Senate Committee on Foreign Relations, Assistant Secretary of State Holdridge stated that the U.S. commitment to reduce arms sales to the ROC was predicated upon a continued peaceful approach by the PRC toward the ROC. Beijing's leaders denied that its statement of seeking a peaceful solution to the Taiwan question represented any commitment to the United States. The PRC insisted that to predicate U.S. arms sales upon Beijing's peaceful solution to the Taiwan issue would be premeditated interference in the PRC's internal affairs.[33] According to the PRC's interpretation, the term *final resolution* certainly implied that U.S. arms sales to Taiwan must be completely terminated over a period of time. In the opinion of State Department officials, however, that term should not be read as synonymous with ultimate termination of U.S. arms sales to the ROC; it referred rather to resolving the differences between Washington and Beijing on this issue. They argued that the communiqué neither provided for termination of arms sales to the ROC nor specified the time and form that a resolution of these differences must take. These conflicting interpretations demonstrated that the dispute over arms sales to the ROC was not resolved but merely postponed.

Immediately after the communiqué, both the Senate Committee on Foreign Relations and the House Committee on Foreign Affairs held hearings to learn from the administration how it justified this new policy decision. Members of the Senate Committee criticized the new policy. Senator Glenn said that in his considered judgment the communiqué "does undermine the spirit and intent" of the TRA.[34] Senator Jesse Helms contended that the TRA allowed sales to go up and down, depending on need, but the restriction in the communiqué was a one-way street—down.[35]

The House Committee on Foreign Affairs heard from Holdridge an explanation of the provisions in the communiqué and did not express any objections. Indeed, Representative Jonathan Bingham even commended Holdridge for doing a good job. He acknowledged that he had not been consulted on the communiqué, but he had no complaints, he said, because he was not on the Subcommittee on Asian and Pacific Affairs.[36] Bingham's attitude is quite revealing. It shows that many Committee members did not monitor the TRA unless they happened also to be members of the Subcommittee.

In September 1982, the Senate Subcommittee on Separation of Powers of the Committee on the Judiciary held hearings on arms sales to the ROC. Both Chairman John P. East and witnesses outside the administration maintained that the communiqué was in conflict with the TRA. Senator East suggested that President Reagan issue a memorandum or an executive order to the administrative agencies concerned, stating that his administration would sell arms to the ROC in accordance with the TRA provisions. His suggestion was not accepted.

In fairness, it must be said that, in addition to the six assurances previously mentioned, the Reagan administration did take several steps to limit the damage caused by the communiqué with respect to arms sales to the ROC. First, the Reagan administration indexed arms sales to Taipei to account for inflation. In March 1983, Washington revealed that, for purposes of complying with communiqué provisions, in FY 1983 arms sales to the ROC would amount to $800 million, and in FY 1984 the sales level would drop to $780 million. These figures are well above the $600 million in sales for FY 1982 and $295 million in FY 1981. The State Department explained that future arms sales to the ROC would be indexed for inflation, that FY 1979 was established as the base year against which reduced sales would be calculated, and that, by allowing for inflated values of weapons and dollars, the 1979 sales level of $598 million would be converted to $830 million in 1983 dollars. The United States has reduced arms sales to the ROC annually by $20 million (see table on p. 100), but presumably allowances could be made for future inflation.[37]

In July 1983, the United States sold some weapons long awaited by the ROC. These included SM-I standard missiles for ship-borne air defense and AIM-7F Sparrow air-to-air missiles. In June 1984, the United States announced the sale of twelve C-130H transport planes to Taipei to replace obsolete planes. In June 1985, 262 Chaparral surface-to-air missiles were transferred to the ROC to replace obsolete M42 air defense guns. These arms sales show that, according to Washington's interpretation of the communiqué provisions, new models of arms could be sold to Taipei to replace obsolete models.

The Reagan administration has reportedly transferred to the ROC the military technology necessary for developing indigenous fighter planes and warships. In 1986, U.S. firms were helping the ROC to develop an indigenous fighter plane. In mid 1987, the United States sold the ROC blueprints and data packages necessary to build the FFG-7 Oliver Hazard Percy–class frigate. Beijing naturally protested these transactions and accused the United States of violating the August 17 communiqué by transferring military technology to Taiwan.[38] The Reagan administration rejected those protests, maintaining that the communiqué dealt with arms sales, not technology transfers.[39] In a note sent to Beijing in mid August, 1986, the administration further clarified its position, declaring that the communiqué stood on its own and that there was no need to reinterpret it or renegotiate it.[40]

These measures helped to restore mutual trust between Taipei and Washington.

The Henry Liu Case

Improved relations made it possible for the United States and the ROC to work together when the murder of Henry Liu became a crisis. Henry Liu, a Chinese-American and a political writer for the *San Francisco Journal*, was killed on October 15, 1984, in the garage of his home in Daly City, California. Shortly before his death, he had published a biography that was critical of the ROC's late President Chiang Ching-kuo. His death naturally led to the suspicion that it was a political murder. The ROC government took steps to show that its officials had never plotted the murder. On November 12, 1984, it launched a national campaign to round up leading gang members. Among them were Ch'en Ch'i-li and Wu Tun, who confessed that they killed Liu. On November 17, Taipei informed Washington that the killers were members of the United Bamboo gang, whose headquarters was in Taiwan, and that one of the killers, Tung Kuei-sen, had escaped abroad.[41]

The rumor soon spread that there was a close working relationship between the gang and the ROC government, that the gangsters killed Liu at the behest of the ROC Military Intelligence Bureau, and that Chiang Hsiao-wu, son of the late President Chiang, ordered the killing.

Chiang denied any involvement, and so did the ROC government. In February 1985, however, the government charged Chen, Wu, and Vice-Admiral Wang Hsi-ling, former director of the Military Intelligence Bureau, with murder. Two of Wang's deputies, Hu Yi-min and Ch'en Hu-men, were also charged with assisting in the murder.[42]

The case strained Taipei-Washington relations. The U.S. Congress passed a nonbinding resolution calling for the extradition of some of the defendants to stand trial in the United States. The ROC government turned down the request for the extradition because it had no extradition treaty with the United States, and ROC law prohibited extraditing its citizens in the absence of such a law. The United States argued that without diplomatic relations the question of extradition under a diplomatic treaty was irrelevant and should not present an obstacle to having Chen and Wu's case handled in U.S. courts. Taipei had previously proposed an extradition agreement with Washington so that ROC economic criminals who fled to the United States could be brought back to Taipei for trial. The United States had rejected that proposal. Therefore, Taipei's refusal to extradite Chen and Wu was legally and morally justified. Nevertheless, the ROC's refusal prompted suggestions in the U.S. Congress that $760 million of arms sales provided to Taipei in 1985 could be adversely affected.

Taipei took steps to defuse many of the political concerns that had arisen between the United States and the ROC. Its justice system publicly tried the defendants so that the true facts of the case could be reported. It allowed Jerome Cohen, representing Liu's widow, to take part in the trials.[43] A police officer from Daly City was permitted to have seventeen hours to interrogate the defendants.[44] By early April 1985, Ch'en Ch'i-li and Wu Tun were convicted and sentenced to life imprisonment. Two weeks later, the military court also sentenced Wang to life imprisonment. Two of his deputies were given prison terms of two and one-half years. Taipei demonstrated its willingness to deliver justice swiftly and without regard for the defendants' official status.

The U.S. State Department from the very beginning discounted the possibility that officials in the ROC government were involved in the crime. It also announced that the ROC authorities had cooperated fully with the United States in the murder investigation.[45] In June,

Senator Jeremiah A. Denton wrote President Reagan that the open trials had uncovered the facts of the murder and that, since there was no
extradition agreement between the United States and the ROC, and
since the law in California prohibited trying defendants twice for the
same act, it would be inappropriate for the U.S. government to extradite them for another trial in the U.S. court.[46] The Reagan administration thereafter did not press Taipei to extradite the defendants in its
custody. Tung Kuei-sen was finally extradited to the United States
from Brazil and in May 1988 was given a prison term of 27 years. The
murder case was thus closed.

Cultural and Commercial Relations

Breaking diplomatic relations between Washington and Taipei has
never harmed cultural and commercial relations, which are in fact authorized and encouraged by the TRA.

Since 1979, more than 60 agreements on cultural relations have
been signed between the CCNAA and the AIT. A large number of
U.S. scholars and experts have visited the ROC during the 1980s. The
Nobel laureate in economics for 1979, John W. Schultz, came to Taiwan in December 1980. In July 1982, another Nobel laureate for economics (1980), Lawrence Klein, led a group of scholars to lecture in
the ROC. Since 1979, more than one hundred college and university
presidents have visited Taiwan.

International conferences have been an important vehicle for U.S.-
ROC cultural relations. The most important of these conferences is
probably the annual Sino-American Conference on Mainland China.
Attended by over one hundred Chinese and U.S. scholars, it rotates
between the United States and the ROC every other year.

Each year, more than two thousand ROC students go to the
United States for advanced studies. ROC students have now totaled
over 23,000, surpassing in number all other foreign students in the
United States. About five hundred U.S. students come to study in
Taiwan each year.[47]

Despite the absence of diplomatic relations between the ROC and
the United States, commercial relations have prospered as never before. Bilateral trade increased from $9 billion in 1979 to $31 billion in
1987. The U.S. share of the ROC's total trade rose from 29 percent in
1979 to 35 percent in 1987. U.S. investment in the ROC also jumped
from $181 million in 1979 to $2.46 billion in 1988.[48]

In recent years, however, trade has become a serious problem between the ROC and the United States because of two developments.

The first is the growing U.S. trade deficit with the ROC. That deficit increased from $2.3 billion in 1979 to $16 billion in 1987.[49] The other is a growing concern among the U.S. public that the U.S. trade imbalance with the rest of the world is one of the most important problems facing the domestic economy. The U.S. Congress has responded to demands from the public for tough action. As a result, the Reagan administration imposed heavy pressure on the ROC to rapidly open its domestic market and to appreciate its currency.

The ROC did not act fast enough to correct the trade imbalance with the United States, probably because its officials did not perceive it to be such a serious problem and Taipei was reluctant to take drastic measures for fear of economic recession and political instability. In 1987 and 1988, however, the ROC appreciated its currency by 40 percent and opened its market to U.S. beer, wine, beef, poultry, banking, insurance, credit cards, and other services in which the United States has a competitive edge. Taipei also reduced or eliminated tariffs and quantitative restrictions on thousands of products. The ROC has also tried to reduce its exports to the United States while encouraging imports from the United States. Its officials hope that the country's trade surplus in 1988 will be reduced to about $9 billion.

The absence of diplomatic relations has not prevented trade officials of the United States and the ROC from having face-to-face negotiations. At first, U.S. officials would take part in trade talks held in Taipei as advisers to AIT officials so that the talks could be called unofficial. They also preferred not to be covered by local mass media. In recent years, they stopped pretending that they were not chief negotiators on the U.S. side, and the negotiations are closely watched by the press.

The most recent controversial trade issue has been the importation of turkey meat. Since the ROC decided to open its market to U.S. whole turkeys, a small war has been raging on the domestic agricultural front, with local poultry farmers firing protests to the AIT and the ROC trade office. On May 20, 1988, an eighteen-hour demonstration by farmers and sympathizers ended in widespread destruction of property, both public and private, shocking a broad spectrum of the population. The United States wanted to export not only turkey meat but also various waste turkey parts, such as internal organs. Washington has backed its demand by threatening to invoke Section 301 of the U.S. Trade Act of 1974.

The ROC is committed to an open market philosophy, and it has been more cooperative than South Korea and Japan in seeking to reduce the trade surplus with the United States. However, as the ROC

has become more democratic, the government is less free to make
trade concessions to the United States because of the strong opposition from the interest groups that are likely to suffer. Its officials hope
that mutual understanding and good will can endure on both sides,
whatever trade conflicts there may be, and that these issues can be
settled amicably.

Conclusion

The U.S. decision to break diplomatic relations
with the ROC was undertaken in haste and in total secrecy. It left
U.S.-ROC relations in a state of disorder and uncertainty and placed
the ROC in a real crisis. On December 30, 1978, President Carter
issued a memorandum for all departments and agencies to take steps
to maintain U.S.-ROC relations.[50] Being only an executive decree,
the memorandum could not adequately deal with the many complex
legal issues. The TRA filled a legal void and provided a new framework for conducting relations. The Act may also provide the ROC
with stronger security assurances than were provided in the mutual
defense treaty of 1954 because boycotts and embargoes are now considered, and these were not identified in the treaty.

As a new law, the TRA stipulates only in general terms some
principles for maintaining U.S.-ROC relations. As a compromise between the executive branch and the Congress, it represents a remarkable collaboration based on compromise. Yet the implementation of
the TRA ultimately depends on the good faith and careful concern of
the executive branch. The Carter administration used various means
to downgrade U.S.-ROC relations. That administration's hostile attitude toward the TRA and the new mutual distrust between Washington and Taipei that immediately surfaced left bilateral relations cool
and tense.

President Reagan's personal wish to strengthen the TRA was
hampered by his administration's eagerness to reach an accommoda-
tion with the PRC for strategic reasons. Eventually, mutual trust between the United States and the ROC was gradually restored. For
example, improved communication between Washington and Taipei
enabled both sides to resolve the complex problems that erupted after
the murder of Henry Liu in October 1984 at Daly City, California.
These same communication links defused the potential crises over the
disappearance of Colonel Chang Hsien-yi, a nuclear scientist working
at the Chungshan Institute of Science and Technology who had been

reportedly spirited out of Taiwan in January 1988 by the CIA with blueprints of sophisticated nuclear missiles being developed at the Institute.

The Reagan administration has a mixed record of implementing the TRA. The 1982 communiqué violated the provisions of the TRA. It never settled the issue of U.S. arms sales to the ROC, and it has greatly damaged Taiwan's security.

U.S.-ROC cultural and commercial relations have kept expanding. Although the U.S. trade deficit has become a contentious issue with political implications, political passions should not be allowed to use the TRA to punish the ROC for the U.S. foreign trade problem.

Bipartisan congressional support produced the TRA, and that law should survive as administrations change during the next decades. Pressed to rely more on its own resources, the ROC still hopes that the TRA will remain in force and be implemented more faithfully than before. The ROC has tried very hard to win good will and understanding from the U.S. Congress so that political pressures will not alter the TRA to Taipei's disadvantage and harm U.S.-ROC relations. For example, the ROC has invited senators, congressmen, their wives, and their key staff to Taiwan. From 1981 to 1987, more than 35 senators and 130 congressmen visited the ROC. During that same period, an average of ten groups of congressional staffs came to Taiwan. To influence U.S. public opinion favorably toward the ROC, Taipei has also invited many state governors, state legislators, and religious, cultural, and social leaders for get-acquainted visits. Former senior governmental officials, such as William P. Clark, Robert C. McFarlane, and Caspar Weinberger, have been guests of the ROC government.

In spite of the vigorous efforts of the ROC to cultivate members of Congress, congressional oversight of the implementation of the TRA has left much to be desired. Some special mechanism should be set up to supervise more effectively the implementation of the TRA. During the debate on the enactment of the TRA, the Congress rejected a proposal for establishing a select committee to oversee the implementation of the TRA, on the grounds that existing congressional committees could do the job. In view of the fact that these committees were sometimes too busy to supervise the implementation of the TRA, Congress should perhaps reconsider establishing a select committee or subcommittee for just that purpose.

Notes

1. *Department of State Bulletin*, 79, no. 2022 (January 1979): 25.

2. *China News* (Taipei), December 30, 1979.

3. *Department of State Bulletin*, 79, no. 2022 (January 1979): 25.

4. See, for example, Lester L. Wolff and David L. Simon, eds., *Legislative History of the Taiwan Relations Act* (Jamaica, N.Y.: American Association for Chinese Studies, 1982); Robert L. Downen, *The Taiwan Pawn in the China Game: Congress to the Rescue* (Washington, D.C.: Georgetown University, Center for Strategic and International Studies, 1979).

5. Zbigniew K. Brzezinski, *Power and Principle: Memoirs of the National Security Adviser, 1977–1981* (New York: Farrar, Straus & Giroux, 1983), pp. 209–33.

6. *Department of State Bulletin*, 79, no. 2022 (January 1979): 25.

7. See Document 35 on p. 267 in Hungdah Chiu, *China and the Taiwan Issue*.

8. *Congressional Quarterly. Weekly Report*, 37, no. 6 (February 10, 1979): 260.

9. *Congressional Quarterly. Weekly Report*, 37, no. 10 (March 10, 1979), p. 403.

10. Ibid., pp. 365 and 431.

11. Ibid., p. 404.

12. *Congressional Quarterly. Weekly Report* 37, no. 11 (March 17, 1979), p. 437.

13. Hungdah Chiu, *China and the Taiwan Issue*, p. 268.

14. Ibid., p. 274.

15. *Department of State Bulletin*, 79, no. 2026 (June 1979): 26.

16. U.S. Congress, Senate, *Taiwan: Hearings Before the Committee on Foreign Relations on S. 245, 96th Congress, 1st Session, 1979* (Washington, D.C.: Government Printing Office, 1979), p. 11.

17. U.S. Congress, Senate, *Oversight of Taiwan Relations Act: Hearings Before the Subcommittee on East Asian and Pacific Affairs of the Committee on Foreign Relations, 96th Congress, 1st Session, 1979* (Washington, D.C.: Government Printing Office, 1979), p. 13. (Hereafter cited as *Oversight of TRA*.)

18. Ibid., pp. 15–16.

19. Ibid., p. 15.

20. King-yuh Chang, "Partnership in Transition: A Review of Recent Taipei-Washington Relations," *Asian Survey* 21, no. 6 (June 1981): 619.

21. *Oversight of TRA*, p. 20.

22. Alexander M. Haig, Jr., *Caveat: Realism, Reagan and Foreign Policy* (New York: Macmillan, 1984), p. 200.

23. Ibid., p. 204.

24. *United States Daily News* (Taipei), March 24, 1983.

25. Robert G. Sutter, *The China Quandary: Domestic Determinants of U.S. China Policy, 1972–1982* (Boulder, Colo.: Westview Press, 1983), p. 146.

26. *Washington Post*, June 13, 1980.

27. A. Doak Barnett, *U.S. Arms Sales: The China-Taiwan Tangle* (Washington, D.C.: Brookings Institution, 1982), p. 27.

28. Haig, *Caveat*, p. 208.

29. Ibid., p. 210.

30. Ibid., pp. 195, 211–14.

31. *New York Times*, August 18, 1982.

32. *Report on ROC-U.S. Relations, 1981–1983* (Taipei: Academia Sinica, Institute of American Culture, 1984), p. 129.

33. *People's Daily*, August 17, 1982.

34. U.S. Congress, Senate, *U.S. Policy Toward China and Taiwan: Hearings Before the Committee on Foreign Relations, 97th Congress, 2nd Session, 1982* (Washington, D.C.: Government Printing Office, 1982), p. 3.

35. Ibid., p. 9.

36. Ibid., p. 28.

37. *Washington Post*, March 23, 1983; Robert L. Downen, *The Tattered China Card* (Washington, D.C.: Council for Social and Economic Studies, 1984), p. 82.

38. *Far Eastern Economic Review*, July 24, 1986, p. 27. (Hereafter cited as FEER.)

39. *Washington Post*, April 25, 1986.

40. *FEER*, August 28, 1986, pp. 26–27.

41. *The Central Daily*, February 28, 1985.

42. *The United Daily*, February 5, 1985.

43. *China Times*, March 20, 1985.

44. *China Times*, January 31, 1985.

45. *China Times*, February 16, 1985.

46. *The Youth Daily*, June 9, 1985.

47. *The United Daily*, December 1985.

48. see note 28, Introduction

49. Council for Economic Planning and Development, Republic of China, *Taiwan Statistical Data Book 1988* (Taipei, Taiwan: Council for Economic Planning and Development, 1988) p. 215.

50. *Department of State Bulletin*, 70, no. 2023 (February 1979): 24.

Index